"WHATEVER IT IS, IT'S BETTER AT RATNER'S!"

Now, the internationally famous dairy restaurant reveals its cooking secrets to you.

Over seventy years of excellence in serving the authentic cuisine of a great European tradition is distilled within these pages. Now you can experience that excellence at your own dining table.

THE WORLD-FAMOUS
RATNER'S
MEATLESS
COOKBOOK

THE WORLD-FAMOUS
RATNER'S
MEATLESS
COOKBOOK

Judith Gethers and Elizabeth Lefft

To JACOB HARMATZ,
king of Delancey Street . . . . . .
and other places.

ACKNOWLEDGEMENTS

The authors of this book wish to acknowledge the invaluable assistance of Harold Harmatz, Harold Zankel, Belle Lefft, Abe Goldman, Sam Miner, Morris Brietbart, Helen Feingold and the entire kitchen staff of Ratner's Restaurant.

Without their cooperation this book would not have been possible.

We also wish to give very special thanks to Steven Gethers for his patience and understanding.

TABLE OF CONTENTS

Foreword

The idea for a RATNER'S COOKBOOK was spawned in Paris.

Paris, France, if you will.

We had spent a week in the loveliest of all cities stuffing ourselves from marketplace cafés to gourmet shrines. As a fitting and proper farewell to Gay Paree, we saved the best for last.

On the eve of departure, the distant lights of the Notre Dame Cathedral sparkled in our aperitifs. Several sighs later, the captain was preparing a dish which rivaled anything we'd seen in the Louvre.

We watched.

We drooled.

We smiled at our dining neighbors.

From an adjoining table, a perfectly creased gentleman, American, leaned towards an elderly lady and asked, "Isn't it delicious, Mama?"

Mama seemed to consider her reply with the deliberation of one who'd spent a good part of her life chopping (rather than grinding) her gefüllte fish. When she announced her verdict it rang through the room in accents heavy with memories of long ago pogroms.

"Whatever it is," she said, "it's better in RATNER'S."

And she was right.

And so the book.

Introduction

In the glossary of film terms, an "establishing shot" is defined as: "A long shot at the beginning of a new scene, usually to determine the general area of the action."

Somewhere in the movie, *The French Connection,* an establishing shot of Ratner's restaurant flashes on the screen. The producers of this fine motion picture knew that the appearance of the famous landmark would leave no doubt in the minds of the viewing audience that the general area of the action was the East Side's Delancey Street. For as long as Delancey Street has remained one of New York City's most colorful thoroughfares, Ratner's restaurant has been its primary source of pride and identification. Ask any cab driver to drop you off on "Delancey between Suffolk and Norfolk" and invariably he will counter with "You want Ratner's?" Most people do.

The story of Ratner's is a cavalcade featuring the great and near great, the famous and infamous as well as the average customer who ventures to this East Side land of onion rolls, chopped liver, baked cutlet and incomparable pastries. The original Ratner's began in a small store on Pitt Street in 1905. Located in the heart of the ghetto, it catered primarily to those who had fled Europe for the promises offered by the New World. Serving quality food at reasonable prices (twenty-five

cents for a many-course meal) its meatless cuisine
served as a model for other restaurants. Then, as now,
nothing on its menu contained a meat product. De-
scribed as "Vegetarian-Dairy," its history, like that of
the ancient dietary laws, evolved out of a sense of
safety, cleanliness and expediency. In the early 1900s
when Europeans were emigrating to the United States
in increasing proportions, ethnic restaurants mush-
roomed throughout the Lower East Side of New York
in an effort to accommodate divergent tastes. With no
proper refrigeration and lacking necessary sanitary con-
ditions, many of those who relied on meat products
were soon forced to close shop. Dairy restaurants
proved more sanitary, became popular and in time began to flourish. At first meals were traditional (soup,
gefüllte fish or white fish). But Jacob Harmatz, founder
of Ratner's, predicted that tastes would change, that
food based on blandness offered no lasting appeal. It
had to be imaginative as well as delicious. Before long,
Mr. Harmatz featured new and interesting combinations
which changed "Vegetarian-Dairy" from a description
to an acknowledged form of cuisine.

In 1918 the thriving infant was forced by success to
seek larger and better quarters at 138 Delancey Street,
its present address. Under the expert guidance of Jacob
Harmatz and the brothers Zankel, Max and Louis, the
restaurant grew to heroic proportions, beyond the
dreams of its founders. By the 1920s, Ratner's was
roaring with the rest of the country. The lure of vaudeville at the neighboring Loew's Delancey, superb food
and the possibility of seeing their favorite performers
in the restaurant between shows, brought people to
Ratner's in droves. Customers paused between courses
to stare at the great Al Jolson, the Ritz Brothers,
Fanny Brice and James Barton as they argued the com-
parative merits of Challah *vs.* Onion roll. Even today,
long after the demise of vaudeville, people of the arts
and politics are "regulars" at Ratner's . . . from Molly
Picon sparring in Yiddish with the legendary Ratner's

waiters to the chic Abbe Lane, "Now" Dennis Hopper, hilarious Jackie Mason, wry Dick Gregory, Marty Allen, Henny Youngman, Edie Gormé and Steve Lawrence, David Frye, Sam Levenson, Walter Matthau, Irving Wallace, Elia Kazan, Sam Jaffe, Zero Mostel, Max Gordon, Jascha Heifetz; just a few from the long list of celebrity diners. Ex-Governor Rockefeller followed a tradition of coming to Ratner's on the eve of every election, claiming it's his "good luck" place. (There must be something to it. He's done pretty well at the polls.) Ex-Mayor Lindsay, at his cabinet meetings, was served Ratner's pastries, brought in specially for him and his associates. Bobby Kennedy made several trips to the restaurant. Robert Wagner Sr. was a devotée. Ad infinitum, politics aside.

Today, what once was little more than a tidy nook, is a beautifully decorated, multi-colored establishment which comfortably seats three hundred and fifty people at one sitting. Upstairs (for weddings, Bar Mitzvahs or private parties) an additional one hundred and seventy people have ample space to dine, "Horah" to their hearts' content and partake of the delicacies obtainable only at Ratner's, delicacies which have been acclaimed by literally millions of residents of (and visitors to) New York City. On an average, ten thousand people a week eat in Ratner's; expatriates from the East Side making pilgrimages to Delancey Street— sometimes an individual yielding to a personal nostalgia, most times as a safari "en famille." They come from Park Avenue, Westchester, Des Moines and, yes, even Paris, retaining the images of "Vegetarian-Dairy" dishes, seductive rolls and pastries that created mouth-melting memories. They are pleasantly surprised to find that though the original owners are, alas, long gone, their heirs have retained the standards set for them by their fathers.

Today, Harold Harmatz and Harold Zankel operate the restaurant, adding ingenious touches of their own, acquired over long years of apprenticeship. Of their one hundred employees, some have been part of Ratner's since its inception. Others have been part of it for decades; managers, waiters, chefs, salad men, all dedicated to the concept that the most important entity in any restaurant is FOOD. While elbow room and friendly service have helped build Ratner's into a New York tradition, the preparation and serving of food remains its primary concern. When the facilities were modernized Ratner's theories proved as different and original as its operation. Where other restaurants might have enlarged seating capacity, Ratner's spent a quarter of a million dollars enlarging its kitchens. Although smart new decor, lighting fixtures and upholstering were not neglected, the owners did not add new seats for old kitchens. They added new kitchens to serve the same seating capacity.

America's newly-found preoccupation with ecology and health has, if anything, added to Ratner's clientele. Young people especially, have discovered the joys of meatless meals, fresh fish and green vegetables, a concept of dining pioneered by Ratner's from its beginning.

This cookbook has been a long time in the making. Since all of the recipes were conceived for institutional use, it was not a simple matter to adapt them for home consumption. Long hours were spent in the reduction of these recipes, in their testing, in their tasting, in their perfection. The result is a compilation of more than two hundred and fifty recipes that are easy to prepare, with ingredients that are nutritious, tasty and readily available at your local markets.

RATNER'S RESTAURANT has spent its lifetime serving you. Now, with pride, it comes into your home. Enjoy!!

Glossary of Foods

Babka Sweet yeast dough that can be made into many shapes. It is usually filled with almond paste and sprinkled with streusel.

Bagel A doughnut-shaped roll, sometimes called a "petrified doughnut." Delicious served warm.

Blintz A crêpe-like pancake filled with cheese, fruit or vegetables, rolled and sautéed in butter until golden brown.

Borscht A grated beet soup flavored with lemon or sour salt and served hot or cold.

Bow Ties Noodles shaped like bow ties. Also, a crisp cookie that is shaped like a bow tie.

Challah A braided yeast bread with a cake-like texture resulting from the use of eggs and egg yolks in the dough. It is the traditional Sabbath Night bread.

Charlotte A form of strudel baked in an oblong form and served warm.

Farfel Tiny crumbled pieces of noodles or matzohs.

Frangipane Filling A mixture of almond paste, eggs and sugar used as a filling for cakes, pies and cookies.

Gefüllte Fish Finely chopped or ground raw fish mixed with eggs to make a fish pudding that is shaped into serving-sized pieces. It means "stuffed fish" as years ago the fish was skinned and the skin was stuffed with the chopped fish. Then the whole fish was cooked.

Hamantaschen (Haman's Pockets) Traditional Purim cakes that are shaped into triangles and filled with cooked mashed prunes or a poppy seed combination.

Kuchel An egg-rich dough with fluffy lightness that bakes into a crisp cookie.

Lox Salmon that is smoked or pickled. Either way it is delicious.

Mandelbreit (Almond Bread) A dry, lightly sweet bread that is flavored with almonds. It is usually cut into thin slices and served with tea.

Marmaliga Cornmeal mush that is cooked with butter and milk and served with cottage cheese and/or cream.

Matzoh A thin, unleavened cracker that is used as a bread substitute.

Matzoh Ball A dumpling made of matzoh meal and eggs.

Matzoh Brel Crumbled matzos mixed with eggs and fried in butter, pancake style, until crisp.

Pirogen Circles of dough topped with a variety of fillings such as potato, cheese, cabbage, then folded over into half circles and boiled.

Protose A vegetable protein substitute. It can be found in health-food stores.

Ruggeles Tiny triangles of sweet dough that are filled with fruit, nuts and sugar and rolled to form crescents.

Schmaltz Herring Herring that is packed in brine and usually sold out of a barrel. It is very salty and must be soaked before using.

Shav Sour grass or spinach made into a traditional soup.

Streusel Cake topping made with sugar, flour, butter and almonds.

Strudel A very elastic dough stretched to paper thinness, filled with fruit or cheese and rolled and baked, brushed heavily with butter, until crisp. Best served warm from the oven.

Taiglach Small pieces of cream-puff-like dough baked and then cooked in a honey syrup with candied fruits and nuts. Taiglach are piled into a pyramid on a serving platter. This is a traditional dish for Rosh Hashannah and Purim.

Texured Protein A vegetable protein substitute. It is found in many supermarkets.

Appetizers

The word "Appetizer" means "appetite teaser." At Ratner's we advise our patrons to protect themselves, for nowhere else in the world do appetizers wink so enticingly.

A veritable Jewish antipasto, they run the gamut from chopped liver (vegetarian, of course) to Greek salad or pickled lox.

Made to titillate the most sophisticated of palates, these easily prepared dishes can be arranged to fit the most formal and gracious dining tables or prepared for "shlepping" on picnics.

Delicious.

knishes

⅓ cup egg whites (about 2)	Oil
2 tablespoons oil	Vegetable Filling (Page 2)
¼ teaspoon salt	and/or Potato Filling
¾ cup water	(Page 71)
3 cups all-purpose flour	1 egg, beaten, for wash

1. Combine first 5 ingredients and beat with an electric mixer until smooth. Pour a thin layer of oil over dough. Let stand at room temperature for 1 hour.

2. Prepare filling as directed.

3. Preheat oven to 350° F. (Moderate).

4. On a heavily floured board, knead dough until smooth and elastic. Roll out to a ⅛-inch thickness, shaping into a 14 × 24-inch oblong. Brush dough with oil.

5. Spoon Potato Filling along one 24-inch edge of the dough. Spoon Vegetable Filling along the other 24-inch edge.

6. Roll the dough over the filling and continue rolling towards the center. Then roll the other side towards the center in the same way. Separate the 2 rolls by cutting down the center. Cut each long roll into 2 pieces.

7. Place all 4 pieces on a heavily greased cookie sheet. Brush with oil and bake for 35–40 minutes, or until golden brown.

8. Remove from oven and brush with egg wash. Return to oven and bake 10 minutes longer.

9. Cut into 1½-inch pieces and serve warm.

NOTE: After cooling, knishes may be sliced, wrapped and frozen (up to one year) and used when desired.

Four 12-inch lengths

vegetable filling

¼ cup oil
1½ cups chopped onion
1 clove garlic, chopped
1 carrot, diced
1 cup chopped celery
2 cups chopped mushrooms

½ cup chopped green pepper
1 cup cooked rice
1 cup cooked kashe
1 egg
Salt and freshly ground pepper

1. In a 10-inch skillet heat the oil. Add onion, garlic,

carrot, celery, mushrooms and green pepper and sauté for 10 minutes, or until vegetables are tender.

2. Stir in rice, kashe and egg. Season to taste with salt and pepper.

3. Use as filling for Knishes (Page 1).

3½ cups filling (enough for two 12-inch knishes)

chopped herring

6 large matjes herring fillets or pickled herring fillets	1 tablespoon sugar
3 slices challah	3 tablespoons white vinegar
1 large apple, peeled, cored and diced	Lettuce
	Onion rings (optional)

1. Soak hearing fillets in water to cover overnight.

2. Drain and pat dry.

3. Grind or chop finely herring, challah and apple. Stir in sugar and vinegar. Chill.

4. Serve on lettuce leaves garnished with an onion ring.

Serves 6–8

pickled herring

6 schmaltz herring fillets, skinned	1 tablespoon whole pickling spice
½ cup white vinegar	3 cups water
⅓ cup sugar	

1. Soak fillets in cold water to cover for 1 hour.

2. Drain and place in earthenware or glass bowl.

3. Combine remaining ingredients in a small bowl, stirring until the sugar is dissolved.

4. Pour over herring. Cover and chill, at least over-night.

5. Drain and cut into bite-sized pieces.

NOTE: Herring, without the cream sauce, may be refrig-erated for 2–3 weeks.

Serves 6–8

cream sauce for pickled herring

1 recipe Pickled Herring
1 Bermuda onion, sliced and separated into rings
1 cup sour cream

⅓ cup water
¼ cup white vinegar
1 tablespoon sugar

1. Place bite-sized pieces of pickled herring in a serving dish.

2. Combine remaining ingredients in a bowl and stir until well blended.

3. Spoon sauce over herring.

4. Cover and chill for several hours.

Enough for 1 recipe of Pickled Herring

greek salad

6 matjes herring fillets
1 medium head green cabbage, cored and shredded
1 green pepper, sliced
1 carrot, shredded
1 small onion, sliced
1 cup salad oil

¾ cup white vinegar
½ teaspoon white pepper
¼ cup sugar
1 cup sour cream
½ cup water
Salt to taste
Lettuce
Tomato slices

1. Soak herring fillets in water to cover for several hours. Drain and dice into ½-inch cubes.
2. In a large bowl combine cabbage, green pepper, carrot and onion. Add the herring.
3. In a small bowl combine the remaining ingredients except the salt, lettuce and tomatoes. Pour over salad and toss until well blended. Add salt.
4. Cover and chill for several hours or overnight.
5. Serve on a bed of lettuce garnished with sliced tomatoes.

Serves 6–8

pickled lox

2 pounds fresh boneless salmon
Milk
¾ cup sugar
2 cups white vinegar
½ cup water
3 onions, sliced
1 bay leaf
6 peppercorns
1 tablespoon pickling spice
1 cup sour cream
Chopped dill (optional)

1. Slice salmon into 1-inch pieces. Soak in milk to cover and ¼ cup sugar. Refrigerate for 24 hours.
2. Pour off milk and rinse salmon pieces in cold water. Combine remaining ½ cup sugar, vinegar, water, onions, bay leaf, peppercorns and pickling spice. Pour over salmon pieces. Refrigerate for 5–7 days.
3. After 5–7 days, drain and reserve ½ cup of the marinade and the onions. Mix reserved marinade with sour cream. Add chopped dill. Pour over salmon pieces and mix gently to blend.
4. Serve salmon with onions and sauce spooned over the top.

Serves 8

chopped liver

½ pound lentils
2 cups chopped onion
8 hard-cooked eggs
3 tablespoons oil
1 tablespoon peanut butter

¼ teaspoon white pepper
1 teaspoon salt
Lettuce
Horseradish
Tomato slices

1. Cook lentils according to package directions. Drain.
2. Pour ½ cup onion into bowl. Chop finely lentils and eggs. Add to onions.
3. Sauté remaining onions in half the oil until brown.
4. Mix lentil mixture with sautéed onions, the remaining oil, peanut butter, pepper and salt.
5. Serve on lettuce leaves with white or red horseradish and a slice of tomato.

Serves 4–6

holiday chopped liver

1 cup minced celery
2 onions, minced
½ cup oil
12 hard-cooked eggs
8 ounces walnuts, chopped

Salt and pepper
Lettuce
Horseradish
Tomato slices

1. In a skillet sauté celery and onions in oil until dark brown. Cool.
2. Grind or chop finely eggs and walnuts along with sautéed vegetables.
3. Season to taste with salt and pepper. Chill.
4. Serve on lettuce leaves with white or red horseradish, and a slice of tomato.

Serves 6

chopped eggplant

2 medium eggplants
½ cup oil
2 large onions, chopped
   finely
1 green pepper, chopped
   finely

1 (4-ounce) jar pimientos,
   drained and diced
Juice of 1 lemon
Salt and white pepper to
   taste

1. Preheat oven to 350° F. (Moderate).
2. Bake whole unpeeled eggplants for 1 hour, or until easily pierced. Cool.
3. Peel eggplants and chop finely.
4. In a large skillet heat ¼ cup oil and sauté onions and green pepper until golden brown.
5. Stir in eggplant, remaining ¼ cup oil, pimiento, lemon juice, salt and pepper.
6. Serve cold.

Serves 6–8

chopped eggs and onions

1 Bermuda onion, chopped
6 hard-cooked eggs,
   chopped
¼ cup oil

Salt and white pepper
   to taste
Lettuce
Green pepper rings
Radishes

1. Combine first 4 ingredients and blend thoroughly.
2. Chill until ready to serve.
3. Serve in a mound on lettuce leaves or shredded lettuce, garnished with green pepper rings and radishes.

Serves 6

chopped mushrooms and eggs

1 pound mushrooms
2 teaspoons salt
½ cup chopped Baked
Onions (Page 61)
6 hard-cooked eggs,
chopped

Salt and freshly ground
pepper
Lettuce
Tomato slices
Green pepper rings

1. Chop mushrooms and cover with water. Add salt.
2. Bring to a boil, then lower heat. Simmer for 10 minutes. Drain.
3. Grind or chop finely the mushrooms with baked onions and eggs.
4. Season to taste with salt and pepper.
5. Serve on lettuce garnished with tomato slices and green pepper rings.

Serves 6–8

celery and eggs

2 cups finely chopped
celery and leaves
6 hard-cooked eggs,
chopped
3 tablespoons oil
1 teaspoon salt

¼ teaspoon pepper
1 small onion, chopped
Lettuce
Green pepper rings
(optional)
Radishes (optional)

1. In a small bowl combine first 6 ingredients and mix well.
2. Chill.
3. Serve on lettuce leaves garnished with green pepper rings and radishes.

Serves 6–8

spinach and eggs

1 pound spinach, well-
  trimmed and finely
  chopped
6 hard-cooked eggs,
  chopped
2 tablespoons oil

1 teaspoon salt
¼ teaspoon pepper
Lettuce
Green pepper rings
  (optional)

1. In a small bowl combine first 5 ingredients and mix well.
2. Chill.
3. Serve on lettuce leaves garnished with green pepper rings.

Serves 6–8

chopped salmon and celery

½ cup finely chopped
  celery
1 (1-pound) can salmon,
  drained and flaked
1 tablespoon chopped onion
Juice of ½ lemon
1 tablespoon chopped green
  pepper

½ cup Blender Mayonnaise
  (Page 97), approxi-
  mately
Salt and freshly ground
  pepper to taste
Lettuce
Green pepper rings
Onion rings

1. In a bowl combine first 7 ingredients, gradually adding enough mayonnaise to make a fluffy consistency. Stir to blend well.
2. Serve on lettuce leaves garnished with green pepper rings and onion rings.

Serves 4

Soups

Ratner's Restaurant, caterer to the stars, has created a headliner all its own.

Soup.

Traditionally served before the entrée, Ratner's soup stands on its own merits, a vegetarian gourmet's dream. Rich and hearty, aided by a fresh green salad, chunks of crusty bread (or onion rolls), even the most voracious of appetites may not make it to the fruit and cheese for dessert.

Variety? And how!

Vegetable soup, borscht, shav, barley and mushroom and so many more tucked away between these pages, as ladled by Bridget, Hungary's gift to Ratner's kitchens.

Incidentally, most soups are great pick-me-ups, served in a cup or glass between meals. A refreshing change from coffee or tea.

Bet you never thought of it.

consommé with matzoh balls

1 tomato, chopped
2 onions, quartered
2 parsnips, chopped
1 green pepper, chopped
2 cups chopped celery and leaves
½ cup chopped parsley
¼ cup chopped dill
3 quarts water

Shells from 6 eggs (used in making Matzoh Balls)
1 tablespoon salt
1 tablespoon sweet paprika
¼ teaspoon pepper
1 clove garlic, chopped
½ cup Baked Onions (Page 61)
1 recipe Matzoh Balls (see below)

1. In a large kettle combine tomato, onions, parsnips, green pepper, celery, parsley, dill, water, egg shells, salt, paprika and pepper. Simmer, covered, for 1½ hours.
2. Add garlic and baked onions and simmer for another 15 minutes.
3. Strain the broth into a large saucepan.
4. Add matzoh balls and simmer, covered, for 30 minutes.
5. Serve hot.

Serves 8

matzoh balls

6 eggs
1½ teaspoons salt
½ cup Clarified Butter (Page 96)

1½ cups matzoh meal
¼ teaspoon baking powder
¾ cup water

1. Beat eggs, add salt. While beating, add butter.
2. Add matzoh meal and baking powder and continue to beat until well mixed.

3. Gradually beat in water. Chill for at least 2 hours.

4. Moisten hands and form dough into balls the size of large walnuts.

5. Drop into simmering salted water and cook for 40 minutes.

About 24 small matzoh balls

vegetable soup

8 mushrooms, coarsely chopped
1 cup coarsely chopped parsley
2 onions, chopped
2 green peppers, diced
2 cups diced carrots
2 cups chopped celery and leaves
½ cup dried yellow peas
½ cup dried green peas
½ cup dried Lima beans

¼ cup medium barley
1 small head cauliflower, broken into flowerets
3 quarts water
1 tablespoon salt
1 (1-pound) can cut green beans, undrained*
1 (1-pound) can peas, undrained**
1 cup tomato purée
Fresh ground pepper

1. In a large kettle combine all ingredients except canned green beans and peas, tomato purée, and pepper.

2. Cover and simmer for 1 hour.

3. Stir in remaining ingredients. Correct seasonings, if desired.

4. Simmer another 5 minutes. Serve piping hot.

Serves 8

---

* *½ pound fresh green beans, cut into 1-inch lengths, may be substituted for canned green beans. Add green beans to soup at the beginning of the cooking time.*

** *1 pound fresh peas, shelled, may be substituted for canned peas. Add peas to soup 10 minutes before ready to serve.*

holiday vegetable soup

½ cup chopped dill
½ cup chopped parsley
2 cups finely chopped
  celery
2 green peppers, chopped
  fine
2 onions, chopped

2 tomatoes, chopped
4 carrots, diced
½ pound green beans, cut
  into 1-inch lengths
2 quarts water
1 tablespoon salt
½ teaspoon white pepper

1. In a large kettle combine all ingredients.
2. Bring to a boil, lower heat and simmer for 40
minutes, or until vegetables are tender.
3. Correct seasonings. Serve piping hot.

Serves 8

holiday vegetable soup with matzoh balls

1 recipe Holiday Vegetable
  Soup (see above)

1 recipe Matzoh Balls
  (Page 11)

1. Prepare holiday vegetable soup according to directions.
2. Prepare matzoh balls according to directions.
3. Add matzoh balls to simmering soup. Cover and
simmer for 30 minutes longer.
4. Serve piping hot.

Serves 8

split pea soup

1 tablespoon salt	½ cup chopped green
2 quarts water	pepper
1 cup dried yellow split	1 (1-pound) can tomatoes,
peas	drained and chopped
1 onion, sliced	3 cloves garlic, chopped
½ cup diced carrots	½ cup Baked Onions
½ cup chopped celery	(Page 61)

1. In a large kettle combine all ingredients except baked onions.
2. Bring to a boil, lower heat and simmer, covered, for 1 hour, or until peas are mushy.
3. Press through a strainer or whirl in a blender and pour into a large saucepan.
4. Stir in baked onions and mix well.
5. Serve piping hot.

Serves 8

split pea soup with egg dumplings

3 large eggs	1 recipe Split Pea Soup
1 teaspoon salt	(see above)
¾ cup all-purpose flour	Chopped parsley

1. Combine eggs, salt and flour and beat until smooth. The mixture should be the consistency of sour cream.
2. Prepare split pea soup according to directions.
3. Place egg mixture into a funnel and let drip in small droplets into simmering pea soup.
4. Simmer for 10 minutes.
5. Serve hot sprinkled with chopped parsley.

Serves 8

5. In a bowl mix sautéed onions, brown rice, eggs, salt and pepper. Use mixture to stuff peppers.

6. Place peppers side by side in a baking pan.

7. Spoon sauce over peppers and bake for 1 hour.

8. Serve hot with pan juices spooned over peppers.

Serves 6

stuffed cabbage

1 large head green cabbage	1 egg
1 cup rice	Salt and freshly ground
1 carrot	pepper to taste
1 green pepper	1 recipe Stuffed Green
2 stalks celery	Peppers Sauce (Page 46)
1 onion	¼ cup raisins
6 mushrooms	2 tablespoons honey
¼ cup butter	

1. Core cabbage. Cover with water and boil hard for 30 minutes. Drain and cool.

2. Remove 18 leaves from cabbage and shred 2 cups of remaining cabbage. Slice off hard rib to make leaf easier to roll.

3. Cook rice until tender according to package directions. Drain.

4. Preheat oven to 350° F. (Moderate).

5. Grind or finely chop carrot, green pepper, celery, onion and mushrooms. Sauté in butter until mushy but not brown.

6. Stir vegetables into rice. Stir in egg, salt and pepper to taste.

7. Place one heaping tablespoonful on each cabbage leaf. Fold leaf over filling once, turn in sides of leaf and continue rolling.

8. Spoon 1 cup of the sauce into a 9 × 13 × 2-inch pan. Place cabbage rolls, seam side down, in sauce.

9. Sprinkle raisins, honey and shredded cabbage over top.

10. Pour remaining sauce over cabbage rolls. Cover with foil and bake for 1½ hours.

11. Serve on a heated platter with gravy spooned over cabbage rolls.

18 rolled leaves

vegetable chow mein

½ cup butter
3 large onions, sliced
4 cups sliced celery
1 pound mushrooms, chopped
4 cups water
¼ cup soy sauce
Salt and freshly ground pepper

Paprika
½ cup cornstarch
½ cup water
Brown Rice (Page 56), optional
Crisp Noodles (Page 55), optional

1. In a large saucepan heat the butter and sauté onions until transparent.

2. Add celery, mushrooms, water and soy sauce. Season to taste with salt, pepper and paprika. Simmer for 15–20 minutes, or until vegetables are tender.

3. Combine cornstarch with water. Stir into vegetable mixture and continue to cook, stirring, until thickened.

4. Serve piping hot with Brown Rice and Crisp Noodles.

Serves 6–8

noodle chop suey

¼ cup butter
2 large onions, chopped
6 mushrooms, sliced
2 cups cooked and drained broad noodles

3 cups cooked Basic Kashe (Page 52)
Salt and freshly ground pepper

1. In a 10-inch skillet heat butter and sauté onions until golden brown. Add mushrooms and cook until slightly wilted.

2. Add noodles and mix thoroughly. Continue to cook until noodles are thoroughly coated with butter.

3. Add kashe and cook until kashe is dry and noodles are crispy. Season to taste with salt and pepper.

4. Serve on heated plates.

Serves 4

egg roll

1 recipe Blintz Batter (Page 67)
1 pound Coleslaw (Page 87), squeezed dry
½ cup textured vegetable protein OR ¼ cup protose
3 green olives
1 pimiento pod, chopped
1 (7-ounce) can tuna, packed in water, drained and flaked
1 tablespoon soy sauce
⅓ cup oil
English Mustard (Page 99)

1. Prepare blintz batter as directed. Make blintz pancakes and reserve.

2. Combine remaining ingredients, except for the oil and mustard, in a bowl. Blend thoroughly.

3. Place about 2½ tablespoons of mixture into each blintz pancake. Shape as for blintzes.

4. In a skillet heat oil and slowly sauté egg rolls, about 10 minutes, until golden brown on all sides. (Egg rolls may also be fried in deep fat or oil heated to 360° F. for about 5–6 minutes.)

5. Serve hot accompanied by English Mustard.

24 egg rolls

stuffed turkey neck

1 recipe Blintz Batter
  (Page 67)
1 cup fine grits
2 eggs
¾ cup melted butter
2 cups water
1 onion, chopped
1 carrot, diced
½ cup minced celery

6 large mushrooms,
  chopped
1 clove garlic, chopped
½ cup textured vegetable
  protein or ¼ cup
  protose
Salt and freshly ground
  pepper

1. Prepare blintz batter as directed. Make blintz pancakes and reserve.
2. Combine grits and 1 egg.
3. In a skillet heat ½ cup butter and add grits mixture. Cook, stirring, until grits are golden brown.
4. Add water to skillet, cover, and simmer until liquid is absorbed and grits are tender, about 15 minutes.
5. In another skillet heat the remaining ¼ cup butter and sauté onion, carrot, celery, mushrooms and garlic for about 5 minutes. Stir in vegetable protein or protose, remaining egg, grits, and salt and pepper to taste.
6. Put turkey neck together as in egg roll recipe (Page 49) and fry according to directions.

24 pancakes

meatless burgers

1 pound lentils
2 tablespoons butter
1 large onion, chopped
1 cup textured vegetable
  protein OR ½ cup protose
4 eggs

Salt and freshly ground
  pepper
Matzoh meal
½ cup Clarified Butter
  (Page 96)

1. Cover lentils with boiling salted water and simmer until lentils are tender, about 1 hour. Drain.

2. Heat butter in a skillet and sauté onion until tender. Place in a bowl.

3. Add lentils, vegetable protein or protose, eggs, salt and pepper. Knead with hands to mix well.

4. Shape into 6 patties. Roll patties into matzoh meal to coat completely.

5. Heat clarified butter in a skillet and brown patties evenly, about 5 minutes on each side.

6. Serve hot.

6 burgers

meatless chops

6 hard-cooked eggs	1 cup half and half
¼ cup butter	3 eggs
1 large onion, chopped	Salt and pepper to taste
½ cup minced celery	2 cups matzoh meal
1 cup instant mashed potato granules	½ cup Clarified Butter (Page 96)

1. Chop eggs and place in a bowl.

2. In a skillet heat butter and sauté onion and celery until golden brown. Add to chopped eggs.

3. Add potato granules, half and half, 2 eggs, beaten, and salt and pepper.

4. Shape into 6 patties resembling lamb chops.

5. Beat remaining egg. Dip patties into egg and then into matzoh meal, coating thoroughly.

6. Heat clarified butter in a skillet and brown chops evenly, about 5 minutes on each side.

7. Serve hot.

6 chops

basic barley

2 cups medium barley	¼ teaspoon pepper
1 egg	¼ cup butter
Salt	4 cups boiling water

1. In a bowl mix barley, egg, 2 teaspoons salt and pepper.
2. Heat butter in a skillet and sauté barley mixture until brown.
3. Add water, cover tightly and simmer for 30–40 minutes, or until liquid is absorbed and barley is tender but still firm.
4. Season to taste with salt and serve hot.

Serves 6

barley with onions

¼ cup butter	1 recipe Basic Barley
2 large onions, chopped	(see above)

1. Heat butter in a skillet and sauté onions until golden brown.
2. Prepare barley according to directions. Stir into onions and cook until heated through.
3. Serve hot.

Serves 6

basic kashe

1½ cups kashe	3 cups boiling water
2 eggs	2 teaspoons salt
2 tablespoons butter	

1. In a bowl mix kashe and eggs.

2. Heat butter in a large skillet. Add kashe and cook, stirring, until kashe is lightly browned and crumbly.

3. Heat water and salt in a large saucepan. Pour in kashe.

4. Simmer, covered, over low heat for 30 minutes, stirring occasionally, until liquid is absorbed and kashe is fluffy.

Serves 6

noodle farfel

2 cups noodle farfel OR   Dash of pepper
  matzoh farfel   ¼ cup butter
2 eggs, well beaten   2 cups water
1 teaspoon salt

1. In a bowl mix farfel, eggs, salt and pepper.

2. Heat butter in a skillet and sauté farfel mixture until brown and crumbly.

3. Add water, cover tightly and simmer for 10–15 minutes, or until liquid is absorbed.

4. Serve hot.

Serves 6

noodle farfel with onions

2 cups noodle farfel OR   Dash of pepper
  matzoh farfel   ½ cup butter
2 eggs, well beaten   2 cups water
1 teaspoon salt   1 large onion, chopped

1. In a bowl mix farfel, eggs, salt and pepper.

2. In a skillet heat ¼ cup butter and sauté farfel mixture until brown and crumbly.

3. Add water, cover tightly and simmer for 10–15 minutes, or until liquid is absorbed.

4. While farfel is simmering, heat remaining ¼ cup butter in a skillet and sauté onions until golden brown.

5. When all the liquid in the farfel mixture has been absorbed, add the onions and mix well.

6. Serve hot.

Serves 6

potato noodles

4 potatoes, quartered	3 cups all-purpose flour
2 eggs, beaten	(approximately)
Salt	1 cup melted butter

1. Cook potatoes in water to cover, about 20 minutes. Drain and cool to lukewarm. Peel.

2. Mash or press potatoes through a food mill or potato ricer.

3. Stir in eggs, 1 teaspoon salt and enough flour to form a stiff dough.

4. Turn out onto a heavily floured board and knead until smooth and elastic, about 5 minutes. (It may be necessary to add more flour as potatoes vary in moisture and egg sizes vary.) Cut dough into quarters.

5. On a heavily floured surface roll out one quarter of the dough until paper thin.

6. With a sharp knife or pizza cutter cut dough into ½-inch strips. Cut strips into 4-inch lengths.

7. Place noodles separately on a floured cloth. Repeat, using remaining dough. Let dry for several hours.

8. Drop noodles into boiling salted water. When noodles rise to surface, drain.

9. Toss with melted butter. Season to taste with salt and serve at once.

Serves 6

potato noodles with fried onions

1 recipe Potato Noodles   4 large onions, sliced
  (Page 54)   Salt and freshly ground
1 cup butter   pepper

1. Prepare potato noodles according to directions.
2. In a large skillet heat butter and sauté onions until golden brown.
3. Toss noodles with onions, adding salt and pepper to taste.
4. Serve hot.

Serves 6

crisp noodles

1 (1-pound) package wide   Oil for deep frying
  noodles

1. Cook noodles according to package directions. Drain. Dry noodles on absorbent paper.
2. In a pan heat oil to 360° F. Drop noodles into the oil, a few at a time, and fry until golden brown, about 2–3 minutes. Remove and drain on absorbent paper. Repeat using remaining noodles.
3. Noodles should be crisp when served. May be served as an accompaniment to Vegetable Chow Mein (Page 48), if desired.

Serves 6–8

matzoh balls with fried onions

1 recipe Matzoh Balls   ¼ cup butter
  (Page 11)   2 large onions, chopped

1. Prepare matzoh balls according to directions. Shape dough into balls the size of a small walnut.

2. Cook in boiling salted water as directed in recipe and drain.

3. In a 10-inch skillet heat butter and sauté onions until golden brown.

4. Add matzoh balls and stir carefully until well coated and heated through.

5. Serve warm.

Serves 6

ratner's special rice

1½ cups raw rice	¼ cup butter
1 cup milk	Salt

1. Cook rice in boiling salted water according to package directions.

2. Drain, add milk and simmer, stirring occasionally, until milk is absorbed, 10–15 minutes.

3. Stir in butter. Season to taste with salt.

4. Serve hot.

Serves 6

variations

1. Sprinkle with grated Parmesan cheese.
2. Blend in 1 cup Baked Onions (Page 61).
3. Top with ½ cup sautéed mushrooms.
4. Sprinkle with 4 tablespoons sugar, ¼ teaspoon nutmeg and ¼ teaspoon cinnamon.

brown rice

6 cups water	2 cups brown rice
2 teaspoons salt	¼ cup butter

1. Bring water to a boil and add salt. Add rice and simmer, stirring occasionally, for 45 minutes, or until rice is tender. Drain.

2. Stir in the butter and mix well.

3. Serve on a heated platter. May be served as an accompaniment to Vegetable Chow Mein (Page 48), if desired.

Serves 6–8

asparagus, italian style

2 pounds asparagus
1 (14-ounce) jar spaghetti sauce, heated

1 cup (4 ounces) grated white Cheddar cheese

1. Cook asparagus in boiling salted water to cover until tender, 10–15 minutes. Drain and place on a heat-proof platter.

2. Spoon hot spaghetti sauce over asparagus.

3. Sprinkle with cheese and broil until cheese melts and is bubbly.

4. Serve immediately.

Serves 6

sweet and sour beets

2 (1-pound) cans sliced beets with juice
2 tablespoons cornstarch

Juice of 1 lemon
2 tablespoons sugar
1 teaspoon salt

1. Drain juice from beets into a saucepan.

2. Stir in cornstarch.

3. Cook, stirring, over low heat until sauce bubbles and thickens.

4. Stir in lemon juice, sugar, salt and beets. Heat until bubbly, stirring occasionally.

Serves 6

glazed carrots

6 large carrots   ½ cup brown sugar, firmly
¼ cup butter   packed

1. Scrape carrots and cut into ¼-inch slices.
2. Cover carrots with salted water and cook until half done. Drain.
3. In a large skillet heat butter and stir in brown sugar.
4. Add carrots and cook, covered, over moderate heat until carrots are tender.
5. Uncover and continue cooking until carrots are glazed.
6. Serve immediately.

Serves 4

stewed eggplant

2 medium-sized eggplants   3 large tomatoes, chopped
2 tablespoons butter   1 clove garlic, chopped
½ pound mushrooms,   Salt and freshly ground
  sliced   pepper

1. Preheat oven to 350° F. (Moderate).
2. Bake whole eggplants for 1 hour, or until tender. Cool.
3. Peel and mash or chop eggplant.
4. In a 10-inch skillet heat butter and sauté mushrooms, tomatoes and garlic.
5. Stir in eggplant. Season to taste with salt and pepper.
6. Serve hot or cold.

Serves 6

baked eggplant

2 medium-sized eggplants	Flour
Salt and white pepper	Oil
2 eggs, well beaten	

1. Preheat oven to 400° F. (Hot).
2. Peel and slice eggplant into ½-inch round slices. Sprinkle with salt and pepper.
3. Dip slices into eggs and then dredge in flour.
4. Pour oil to a depth of ¼ inch into two 15 × 10-inch baking dishes and set slices of eggplant in dishes.
5. Bake for 10 minutes until brown on one side. Turn and bake another 10 minutes until brown on the other side.
6. Serve immediately.

Serves 6

variations

1. Place American cheese slices over eggplant when both sides are brown. Bake another 2 minutes, or until cheese melts slightly.
2. Sauté 4 onions, chopped, in ½ cup butter until golden brown. Spoon onions over eggplant slices after they are brown and are ready to be served.

eggplant parmesan

2 medium-sized eggplants, peeled	3 cups (bottled) spaghetti sauce
2 eggs	1 cup grated Parmesan cheese
2 teaspoons salt	
2 cups matzoh meal	2 cups shredded mozzarella cheese
1 cup oil	

1. Cut eggplant into ¾-inch slices.
2. In a bowl beat eggs and salt. Dip eggplant slices into egg mixture. Coat slices with matzoh meal.
3. Fry eggplant slices in oil for 2 minutes on each side. Drain on absorbent paper.
4. Preheat oven to 400° F. (Hot).
5. Place slices side by side in a shallow pan. Top with spaghetti sauce and sprinkle with cheeses. Bake for 10 minutes until sauce is hot and cheese melted.
6. Serve immediately.

Serves 6

fried eggplant

2 medium-sized eggplants   Matzoh meal
Salt and white pepper   Oil
2 eggs, well beaten

1. Peel eggplant and cut into ½-inch slices. Sprinkle slices with salt and pepper.
2. Dip eggplant slices into eggs. Then dredge in matzoh meal.
3. Heat ½ inch oil in a skillet. Brown eggplant for 2 minutes on each side, turning once.
4. As eggplant is fried, place on cookie sheet in a 250° F. oven to keep warm.
5. Serve hot.

Serves 6

stewed mushrooms

¼ cup butter   1 teaspoon sugar
12 medium-sized mush-   1 teaspoon salt
  rooms, sliced   1 teaspoon mushroom
¼ cup all-purpose flour   powder or finely ground
1 cup half and half   dried mushrooms

1. Heat butter in a saucepan and sauté mushrooms until slightly wilted.

2. Sprinkle mushrooms with flour. Gradually stir in half and half.

3. Add sugar, salt and mushroom powder. Cook, stirring, until sauce is thickened.

4. Serve immediately.

Serves 4

broiled mushrooms on toast

16 large mushrooms
¼ cup Clarified Butter
(Page 96)
Salt and freshly ground
pepper

4 slices Challah (Page 106)
Finely chopped parsley and
dill

1. Wash mushrooms and remove stems. (Reserve stems for use in other recipes such as Vegetable Soup.)

2. Place mushrooms on a broiler pan, stem side up, and dot with butter. Sprinkle with salt and pepper.

3. Broil mushrooms until tender, about 5 minutes.

4. Toast challah and place on heated individual serving plates.

5. Arrange mushrooms on toast, stem side down. Serve at once sprinkled with finely chopped parsley and dill.

Serves 4

baked onions

1 cup Clarified Butter
(Page 96)

3 pounds onions, peeled and
sliced

1. Preheat oven to 350° F.(Moderate).

2. Stir butter into onions in a 9 × 13-inch baking pan.

3. Bake for 1½ hours, or until golden brown in color. Stir occasionally.

4. Cool. Refrigerate until needed. (May be stored in refrigerator for up to 2 weeks.)

1 quart

potato pudding

6 potatoes
2 eggs
1½ teaspoons salt
1 cup Baked Onions
  (Page 61)

½ cup all-purpose flour*
¼ teaspoon white pepper
1 teaspoon baking powder

1. Preheat oven to 350° F. (Moderate).

2. Peel and finely grate potatoes into a bowl of cold water. (This removes excess starch from the potatoes and prevents them from becoming soggy.)

3. In another bowl mix eggs, salt, baked onions, flour, white pepper and baking powder.

4. Drain potatoes and press out all liquid. Stir potatoes into batter.

5. Pour batter into a heavily oiled 9 × 13 x 2-inch baking pan. Bake for 1½ hours, or until well browned. (Batter can also be poured into a well oiled 12-cup muffin pan and baked for 40 minutes, OR into two 8-inch pie pans and baked for 1½ hours, or until brown.)

6. Cut pudding into squares and serve hot.

Serves 6–8

---

* At holiday time, matzoh meal may be substituted for flour.

potato chips

6 Idaho potatoes   Salt
Oil for deep frying

1. Peel potatoes. Cut into ⅛-inch slices using the cucumber slicer on your grater.
2. Soak the slices in cold water for 1 hour. (This removes excess starch and makes potatoes stiff rather than soggy.) Drain and dry slices on absorbent paper.
3. Heat oil to 360° F. Drop slices, a few at a time, into oil and fry for 2–3 minutes, or until richly browned. Drain on absorbent paper.
4. Sprinkle with salt to taste.
5. Store in an airtight container in a cool, dry place. Use as you would packaged potato chips.

Serves 6

french fries

6 Idaho potatoes   Salt
Oil for deep frying

1. Cut potatoes into ½-inch slices. Cut each slice into ½-inch strips.
2. Soak slices in cold water for 1 hour. (This removes excess starch and makes potatoes stiff rather than soggy.) Drain and dry slices on absorbent paper.
3. Heat oil to 360° F. Drop slices, a few at a time, into oil and fry for 5–6 minutes. Drain on absorbent paper.
4. Sprinkle with salt to taste.
5. Serve hot with fish or vegetables.

Serves 6

mashed potatoes with fried onions

4 potatoes, peeled and diced   Salt and freshly ground
½ cup heavy cream   pepper
½ cup butter   4 onions, chopped

1. Cook potatoes in boiling salted water until tender,
about 15 minutes. Drain thoroughly and mash.
2. Beat in cream, ¼ cup butter, salt and pepper to
taste. Keep warm.
3. While potatoes are cooking, in a small skillet heat
remaining ¼ cup butter and sauté onions until golden
brown.
4. Mix onions with potatoes and serve on a heated
platter.

Serves 4

browned potatoes

6 large potatoes   2 large onions, sliced
¼ cup oil   Chopped parsley

1. Peel potatoes. Cook in boiling salted water to
cover until tender but still firm, about 30 minutes. Drain.
2. In a 10-inch skillet heat the oil and sauté onions
until golden brown.
3. Dice potatoes and add to onions. Stir gently to
coat all pieces.
4. Fry potatoes, stirring occasionally, until they are
brown and crusty.
5. Serve hot garnished with chopped parsley.

Serves 6

creamed spinach

2 pounds spinach, washed and trimmed	¼ cup butter
1 teaspoon salt	¼ cup flour
	1 cup half and half

1. Cook spinach in water clinging to leaves with salt until tender, about 10 minutes. Cool.

2. Drain spinach and squeeze out all moisture. Reserve ½ cup of the liquid. Chop spinach.

3. In a saucepan melt butter and stir in flour. Gradually stir in half and half and reserved spinach liquid. Cook, stirring, over low heat until sauce bubbles and thickens.

4. Stir spinach into sauce. Correct seasonings.

5. Serve immediately.

Serves 6

Dairy Dishes

The little old lady in Paris who inspired this cookbook must have been talking about the Dairy Dishes.

At Ratner's the pièce de résistance can be blintzes like you never dreamed could happen (plain cheese, filled with fruit or a combination). Freddy has been turning them out for twenty-five years. The pirogen is indescribable so we won't attempt a description. After you make them, *you* tell *us* what they're like. Better brush up on your vocabulary. The pirogen, incidentally, have been hand-fashioned at Ratner's by Esther and Gloria for the last fifteen years. Potato pancakes, noodles with cheese, kashe varnishkes and so many more.

Just one helpful hint. You may not be too familiar with these dishes at first, at least cooking-wise. So if it doesn't look like what you thought it would halfway through, don't start changing things. Follow directions and it will all turn out.

Promise.

blintzes

BATTER

4 eggs	Filling (see below)
2 cups water	⅓ cup Clarified Butter
2 cups sifted all-purpose	(Page 96)
flour	Sour cream (optional)
½ teaspoon salt	

1. In a bowl combine eggs and water and blend thoroughly. Beat in flour and salt. Mixture will be runny.

2. Pour 2 tablespoons of the batter into a hot, greased 7-inch omelet pan. Rotate skillet so bottom of pan is covered evenly.

3. Cook for 3 or 4 minutes on one side, or until golden. Remove from pan and repeat process using all the blintz batter. Pile one on top of the other, uncooked side down. At this point blintz pancake is ready to be filled.

4. Place 2 heaping tablespoons of desired filling on one-half of the unbrowned side of the pancake. Fold pancake over once to cover filling. Fold in sides of pancake. Continue rolling.

5. Heat butter in a skillet until hot. Place blintzes, seam side down, in skillet and sauté until golden on all sides.

6. Serve hot with sour cream.

24 blintzes

cheese filling

2 (8-ounce) packages	¼ cup sugar
farmer cheese	1 teaspoon vanilla
2 egg yolks	

1. In a bowl combine all ingredients and mix thoroughly.
2. Use as filling for blintzes.

blueberry filling

1 (1-pound 5-ounce) can   Grated rind of 1 orange
blueberry pie filling

1. In a bowl combine blueberry pie filling and orange rind. Mix well.
2. Use as filling for blintzes.

apple filling

1 (1-pound 5-ounce) can   Grated rind of 1 lemon
apple pie filling   1 teaspoon nutmeg

1. In a bowl combine all ingredients and mix well.
2. Use as filling for blintzes.

cherry filling

1 (1-pound 5-ounce) can   ½ teaspoon almond extract
cherry pie filling

1. In a bowl combine cherry pie filling with almond extract and mix well.
2. Use as filling for blintzes.

pineapple filling

1 (1-pound 5-ounce) can   ½ cup chopped pecans
pineapple pie filling

1. In a bowl combine pineapple pie filling with pecans and mix well.
2. Use as filling for blintzes.

pirogen dough

3 eggs	4½–5½ cups all-purpose
Oil	flour
2 teaspoons salt	Fillings (Pages 70–72)
1 cup lukewarm water	

1. In a bowl beat together eggs, 2 tablespoons oil, salt and water. Beat in enough flour to form a stiff dough.
2. Knead dough on a floured surface until smooth and elastic. Brush dough with oil to prevent it from drying out and set aside for 1 hour.
3. Knead again and set aside while preparing filling.
4. Roll out half the dough to a ⅛-inch thickness. Cut 3-inch circles with a floured cookie cutter. Repeat until all the dough is used.
5. Put a heaping tablespoon of desired filling in center of circle. Brush edges with water. Fold over circle and pinch edges to secure.
6. Drop pirogen into boiling salted water and cook until they rise to the surface, about 10 minutes. Remove from water and drain thoroughly.*
7. Serve as is or, if desired, drained pirogen may be sautéed in Clarified Butter (Page 96) in a skillet until golden brown.

About 50 small pirogen

---

* Note: After boiling, pirogen may be drained, cooled, wrapped and frozen. To reheat, drop into salted boiling water for 5 minutes to heat through.

kashe filling

¼ cup butter
2 cups chopped onion
1½ cups cooked mashed
    Idaho potatoes
1 egg

3 cups cooked Basic
    Kashe (Page 52)
Salt and freshly ground
    pepper

1. Heat butter in a 10-inch skillet and sauté onion until golden brown.
2. Stir in potatoes, egg and kashe. Heat thoroughly. Season to taste with salt and pepper.
3. Cool.
4. Use as filling for pirogen dough.

Filling for 50 small pirogen

cabbage filling

1 small head green cabbage,
    cored and chopped
Salt
¼ cup butter

2 large onions, chopped
1 (1-pound) can sauerkraut,
    well drained and chopped

1. Sprinkle cabbage with salt and let stand for 2 hours. Drain thoroughly.
2. In a 10-inch skillet heat butter and sauté onion until golden brown. Add cabbage and sauerkraut. Cook, stirring, over low heat for 30 minutes, or until cabbage is tender.
3. Cool.
4. Use as filling for pirogen dough.

Filling for 50 small pirogen

tomato soup

1 (1-pound 12-ounce) can tomatoes, chopped and undrained	1 carrot, diced
	1 quart water
	1 tablespoon salt
2 (1-pound 12-ounce) cans tomato purée	½ teaspoon pepper
	2 tablespoons sugar
1 cup chopped celery	2 egg yolks
1 onion, chopped	1 cup sour cream

1. In a large kettle combine tomatoes, tomato purée, celery, onion, carrot, water, salt, pepper and sugar.
2. Bring to a boil, lower heat and simmer, covered, for 20 minutes.
3. In a small bowl beat egg yolks and sour cream. Gradually add 1 cup hot soup to the egg mixture.
4. Stir the egg mixture into remaining soup and continue stirring—this prevents eggs from curdling.
5. Correct seasonings.
6. Remove from heat and serve immediately.

Serves 8

tomato soup with rice

1 recipe Tomato Soup (see above)	2 cups drained cooked rice

1. Prepare tomato soup according to directions, adding rice to soup just before egg yolks and sour cream are added.
2. Heat for 2 minutes. Beat in egg and sour cream mixture as in tomato soup directions.
3. Remove from heat and serve immediately.

Serves 8

cabbage soup

1 small head green cabbage,
  cored and shredded
1 (1-pound 12-ounce) can
  tomatoes, chopped and
  undrained
2 cups tomato purée
1 quart water

1 tablespoon butter
1 teaspoon sour salt
½ cup sugar
1 tablespoon salt
2 egg yolks
½ cup sour cream

1. In a large kettle combine cabbage, tomatoes, tomato purée, water, butter, sour salt, sugar and salt. Cover and simmer for 45 minutes.

2. In a small bowl beat egg yolks and sour cream. Gradually beat in 1 cup of the hot soup.

3. Stir the egg mixture into remaining soup and continue stirring (this prevents eggs from curdling). Correct seasonings.

4. Remove from heat and serve piping hot. May be topped with a dollop of sour cream, if desired.

Serves 8

mushroom and barley soup

1 (1-pound) can tomatoes,
  chopped
2 quarts water
1 onion, sliced
12 mushrooms, sliced
½ cup chopped celery
½ cup chopped green
  pepper

½ cup diced carrots
½ cup coarse barley
½ cup small dried Lima
  beans
1 cup dried mushrooms
2 tablespoons salt
½ cup Baked Onions
  (Page 61)

1. In a large kettle combine all ingredients except

baked onions. Bring to a boil, lower heat and simmer, covered, for 1½ hours.

2. Stir in baked onions and mix well.

3. Correct seasonings and serve piping hot.

Serves 8

potato soup

6 potatoes, peeled and
  quartered
3 onions, sliced
½ cup diced carrots
½ cup chopped celery
½ cup chopped green
  pepper
½ cup chopped parsley
½ cup tomato juice

2 quarts water
2 tablespoons salt
½ cup Baked Onions
  (Page 61)
1 tablespoon chopped dill
½ cup Clarified Butter
  (Page 96)
½ cup all-purpose flour

1. In a large kettle combine potatoes, onions, carrots, celery, green pepper, parsley, tomato juice, water and salt. Bring to a boil, lower heat and simmer covered, for 40 minutes.

2. Stir in baked onions and dill. Blend thoroughly.

3. In a small skillet heat buttter. Add flour and stir over medium heat until flour is golden brown. Gradually add 1 cup of the hot soup to the flour mixture, stirring constantly.

4. Stir the flour mixture into the remaining soup.

5. Cook, stirring, over low heat until soup bubbles and thickens. Correct seasonings.

6. Serve piping hot.

Serves 8

fish chowder

1 carrot, diced
1 onion, chopped
1 cup diced celery
1 leek, sliced
3 potatoes, diced
1 cup tomato purée
1 teaspoon thyme
1 teaspoon oregano

1 teaspoon salt
1 teaspoon sour salt
6 cups water
1 pound boneless fish fillets,
   diced (carp, whitefish,
   pike, flounder)
Tabasco sauce

1. In a large saucepan combine carrot, onion, celery, leek, potatoes, tomato purée, thyme, oregano, salt, sour salt and water. Cover and simmer for 1 hour, or until vegetables are tender.
2. Add fish and simmer for 15 minutes.
3. Season to taste wth Tabasco sauce. Correct seasonings.
4. Serve piping hot.

Serves 6

cream of barley soup

2 quarts water
1 tablespoon salt
3 tablespoons sugar
1 cup medium barley
1 cup milk

1 cup half and half
½ cup Clarified Butter
   (Page 96)
½ cup all-purpose flour

1. In a large kettle combine water, salt, sugar and barley. Cover and simmer for 1½ hours.
2. Stir in milk and half and half.
3. In a small saucepan heat butter and stir in flour. Add 2 cups of the hot soup to the flour mixture.
4. Stir flour mixture into remaining soup.

5. Simmer, stirring, for 5 minutes. Correct seasonings.
6. Serve piping hot.

Serves 8

rice, kashe or noodle soup

½ cup raw rice or kashe OR   2 tablespoons sugar
   1 cup fine noodles   Salt
4 cups (1 quart) milk

1. Cook rice, kashe or noodles according to package directions. Drain.
2. Place in saucepan and add milk. Heat slowly, stirring occasionally to prevent sticking.
3. Season to taste with sugar and salt.
4. Serve piping hot.

Serves 6

borscht

2 bunches beets, peeled and   2 teaspoons sour salt OR
   grated   juice of 1 medium lemon
3 quarts water   ¾ cup suger
2 tablespoons salt   Boiled potato and sour
                                  cream (optional)

1. Combine all ingredients in a large kettle. Bring to a boil and simmer for 20 minutes, or until beets are tender. Correct seasonings.
2. Serve hot or cold topped with a boiled potato or sour cream.

Serves 8–10

creamy borscht

1 recipe Borscht (Page 19)   Salt and freshly ground
3 eggs   pepper
1 pint sour cream

1. Prepare borscht according to directions.
2. Beat eggs and sour cream in a large bowl. Gradually mix in 2 cups of the hot borscht.
3. Stir the egg mixture into the remaining soup (this prevents the eggs from curdling). Simmer until hot. Do not boil.
4. Season to taste with salt and pepper.
5. Remove from heat and serve hot or cold topped with a dollop of sour cream.

Serves 8–10

shav

2 pounds shav or Swiss   1 cup chopped scallions
  chard leaves, finely   1 tablespoon salt
  chopped   3 eggs
2 quarts water   1 pint sour cream

1. In a large kettle combine shav, water, scallions and salt. Bring to a boil, lower heat and simmer for 15 minutes.
2. Beat eggs and sour cream in a bowl. Gradually beat 1 cup of the broth into egg mixture.
3. Stir this mixture into remaining soup (this prevents eggs from curdling). Stir to blend and remove from heat.
4. Correct seasonings. Serve hot or cold with a dollop of sour cream, if desired.

Serves 8

spinach soup

2 pounds spinach, washed, trimmed and chopped	1 teaspoon sour salt 1 recipe Shav (Page 20)

1. Prepare shav according to directions substituting spinach for shav or Swiss chard and adding sour salt to water.

Serves 8

fruit soup

3 (11-ounce) packages mixed dried fruits	4 blue plums, pitted and quartered
2 quarts water	2 apples, peeled, cored and sliced
1 (1-pound) can pitted red tart cherries, undrained	1 cup sugar
2 pears, cored and diced	Sour cream or unsweetened whipped cream (optional)
2 peaches, pitted and diced	

1. In a large kettle combine dried fruits and water. Simmer until fruits are tender, about 15 minutes.

2. Add remaining ingredients, except cream, and simmer another 5 minutes.

3. Serve hot or cold either plain or topped with a dollop of sour cream or whipped cream.

Serves 8

sour cherry soup

2 (1-pound) cans pitted red tart cherries, undrained	½ cup sugar 1 cup sour cream

1. In a saucepan combine cherries and sugar. Bring to a boil.

2. Lower heat and beat in sour cream.

3. Remove from heat. Serve hot or cold with additional sour cream.

Serves 6

Fish

Ratner's has found the antidote to the unwieldy portable scale and the small print of calorie counters.

Fish.

Our little sea denizens are much in demand. Reason? They are easy on the weight, attractive on the plate and economical with a date. As for their freshness, tomorrow's catch hasn't been hooked yet.

When broiling fish, to eliminate the need for turning the fish, place broiler pan under broiler for 5 minutes, remove from heat, butter well and add fish fillets.

Many of the fish dishes can be partially cooked, cooled, wrapped and frozen. They can be removed from the freezer, defrosted and cooked to desired degree of doneness. But make sure that you use proper wrapping material to protect the food during freezing . . . it must be moisture and vapor proof.

Vito, seventy-five years young and head fish chef at Ratner's for thirty years tells you how to prepare seafood in any style; broiled, boiled, baked, stuffed, fried. You can even do it Italian style if you want to get ethnic about it. With the fish comes but one guarantee. It will be superb.

Viva Vito!

gefüllte fish

STOCK

Fish bones and heads,
  removed from fish
3 quarts water
4 carrots, sliced

1 cup sliced celery
½ cup chopped parsnips
1 large onion, sliced
1 tablespoon salt

FISH

2 pounds boneless yellow
  pike
2 pounds boneless carp
2 pounds boneless white-
  fish*
1 large onion
6 slices challah

½ cup water
1 teaspoon white pepper
1 tablespoon salt
4 eggs
¼ cup oil
Lettuce
Horseradish (optional)

1. In a large kettle combine all stock ingredients and bring to a boil.

2. Grind or chop finely the pike, carp and whitefish several times with the onion and challah.

3. Beat in water, pepper, salt, eggs and oil. Mixture should taste peppery.

4. With wet hands, shape 1 cup of the fish mixture into an egg-shaped ball. Drop into simmering stock. Repeat using remaining fish mixture.

5. Cover and simmer for 1½ hours. Remove fish and place in shallow bowl.

6. Top with carrots in stock.

7. Strain stock over fish. Chill.

8. Serve on lettuce topped with some of the jellied fish broth and carrots. Serve with white or red horse-radish.

Serves 8

---

* Instead of 2 pounds each of the three listed fish, 6 pounds of any assortment of them may be substituted depending upon their availability.

baked gefüllte fish

½ recipe Gefüllte Fish
  (Page 24)
1 recipe Sauce used on
  Baked Fillet of Flounder,
  Spanish Style (Page 32)

1 onion, sliced
1 clove garlic, chopped
3 tablespoons Clarified
  Butter (Page 96)
Paprika

1. Preheat oven to 350° F. (Moderate).
2. Place fish in a 9 × 13-inch baking pan. Combine sauce, onion and garlic and pour over fish.
3. Dot top of fish with butter.
4. Sprinkle fish with paprika and bake, uncovered, for 1 hour.
5. Arrange on a heated platter and serve immediately.

Serves 6

fried herring

12 schmaltz herring fillets
Oil for deep frying

1 large Bermuda onion

BATTER
4 large eggs
½ cup water

¼ cup all-purpose flour

1. Cover herring with water and refrigerate overnight. Drain and pat dry.
2. To prepare batter, in a bowl beat eggs, water and flour until smooth.
3. Dip herring fillets into batter and fry in hot oil (1½ inches deep) untl brown on both sides, about 7–8 minutes.
4. Drain on absorbent paper. Keep warm.
5. Slice onion and separate into rings.

6. Dip onion rings into batter and fry in the same oil as herring fillets until golden brown on both sides, about 2–3 minutes. Drain on absorbent paper.

7. Arrange herring on a heated platter and serve topped with onion rings.

Serves 6

baked herring

12 schmaltz herring fillets (do not remove skin)	¼ cup oil
	1 cup half and half
2 large onions, sliced	Paprika

1. Cover herring with cold water and refrigerate overnight. Drain and wash fillets. Pat dry.

2. Preheat oven to 350° F. (Moderate).

3. Place onions in a 9 × 13 × 2-inch baking pan. Pour oil over onions. Bake for 30 minutes. Drain off oil.

4. Place herring fillets over onions, side by side, in a single layer.

5. Pour half and half over herring and sprinkle with paprika.

6. Bake for 20 minutes. Remove carefully from pan.

7. Arrange on a heated serving platter and serve immediately.

Serves 6

broiled kippered herring

4 kippered herrings	½ cup butter
4 potatoes, peeled and diced	Salt and freshly ground pepper
½ cup heavy cream	4 onions, chopped

1. Remove bones from kippered herring. Place in a broiler pan.

2. Cook potatoes in boiling salted water, about 15 minutes or until tender. Drain and mash.

3. Beat cream, ¼ cup butter, salt and pepper to taste into the mashed potatoes. Keep warm.

4. While potatoes are cooking, in a small skillet sauté onions in remaining ¼ cup butter until golden brown.

5. Broil kippers until hot, about 10–12 minutes.

6. Place kippers on a warm serving platter. Spoon fried onions over the herring and serve with mashed potatoes.

Serves 4

broiled fish

Salmon steak or striped
    bass, flounder or pompano
    fillets
Salt

Pepper
Paprika
Matzoh meal
Oil

1. Grease individual pan and put fish on it.

2. Sprinkle fish with salt, pepper, paprika and matzoh meal.

3. Sprinkle oil over fish and broil about 10 minutes, or until fish flakes easily when tested with a fork. (If fish is to be served with no oil, substitute water and sprinkle over fish to prevent fish from becoming too dry.)

4. Serve immediately.

Individual servings

broiled fish, italian style

6 fish fillets (flounder, pike,
  whitefish or sole)
Matzoh meal
Salt and freshly ground
  pepper

2 tomatoes, chopped
1 clove garlic, chopped
1 onion, sliced
6 mushrooms, sliced
¼ cup oil

1. Dredge fillets in matzoh meal and place in a broiler pan side by side in a single layer. Sprinkle with salt and pepper to taste. Broil lightly until browned, about 10 minutes.

2. Top with garlic and vegetables. Drizzle with oil.

3. Continue broiling until vegetables are lightly browned, about 10 minutes more.

4. Serve immediately on heated individual plates or a hot platter.

Serves 6

broiled pompano with oranges

6 pompano fillets
Salt
Paprika
⅓ cup Clarified Butter
  (Page 96)

4 navel oranges, peeled and
  cut into slices
Chopped parsley

1. Sprinkle fillets with salt and paprika.

2. Place fillets side by side in a single layer in a greased shallow baking pan. Brush with 1 tablespoon butter. Broil until pompano is cooked and flakes easily when tested with a fork, about 15 minutes.

3. Top pompano with orange slices. Brush with remaining butter. Broil another 5 minutes.

4. Arrange on a heated platter. Sprinkle with chopped parsley.

Serves 6

broiled whitefish with dill sauce

3 large whitefish fillets,
  halved crosswise
Salt and freshly ground
  pepper

Lemon juice
¼ cup melted butter
Parsley

SAUCE
⅓ cup butter
⅓ cup all-purpose flour
2 cups milk
1 teaspoon sour salt

2 tablespoons chopped fresh
  dill
Salt and freshly ground
  pepper

1. Sprinkle fillets with salt, pepper and lemon juice.
2. Place fillets side by side in a single layer on a greased shallow pan. Brush with butter and broil until lightly browned, about 15–20 minutes, or until fish flakes easily when tested with a fork.
3. While whitefish is cooking, prepare the sauce. Melt butter in a saucepan. Stir in flour. Gradually stir in milk. Cook, stirring, over low heat until sauce bubbles and thickens.
4. Stir sour salt and dill into sauce. Add salt and pepper to taste.
5. Arrange fillets on a heated platter and spoon sauce over the fish. Garnish with parsley.

Serves 6

broiled brook trout

6 rainbow trout	Salt and freshly ground
¼ cup melted butter	pepper
2 cloves garlic	2 tomatoes, chopped

1. Thaw trout, if frozen. Brush trout inside and out with melted butter.

2. Mash garlic and place inside body cavity of fish.

3. Place on a greased broiler rack side by side. Sprinkle with salt and pepper to taste.

4. Broil until fish is lightly browned, about 10–15 minutes.

5. Turn and sprinkle with tomatoes. Broil again until tomatoes are cooked, about 5–6 minutes, and fish flakes easily when tested with a fork.

6. Arrange trout on a heated platter and serve immediately.

Serves 6

halibut steak with cheese sauce

6 halibut steaks, 1 inch thick	¼ cup melted butter
Salt and freshly ground pepper	Parsley

SAUCE

⅓ cup butter	½ cup sliced green olives
⅓ cup all-purpose flour	(optional)
2 cups milk	Salt and freshly ground
1 cup (4 ounces) grated American cheese	pepper
¼ cup grated Parmesan cheese	

1. Sprinkle halibut steaks with salt and pepper. Brush both sides with melted butter and place in a broiler pan, side by side. Broil until fish is golden, about 10–15 minutes, and flakes easily when tested with a fork.

2. While halibut is broiling, prepare the sauce. Heat butter in a saucepan and stir in flour. Gradually stir in milk. Cook, stirring over low heat until sauce bubbles and thickens. Stir in cheeses. Stir in olives. Season to taste with salt and pepper.

3. With a pancake turner carefully place halibut steaks on a heated platter. Spoon sauce over fish and serve garnished with parsley.

Serves 6

baked fillet or flounder or whitefish

6 flounder or whitefish fillets	Salt

SAUCE

2 teaspoons salt	2 tomatoes, chopped
2 cups water	6 tablespoons Clarified
¼ cup chopped celery	Butter (Page 96)
¼ cup diced carrots	⅓ cup flour
¼ cup chopped green pepper	1 large onion, chopped
	1 clove garlic, chopped

1. Preheat oven to 350° F. (Moderate).

2. Sprinkle fish with salt. Roll up like a jelly roll and place rolls, seam side down, in a shallow baking pan.

3. To prepare sauce, combine salt, water and vegetables in a saucepan. Simmer about 45 minutes, or until vegetables are tender.

4. Heat 4 tablespoons butter in a skillet. Stir in flour and cook until brown. Stir 1 cup of the vegetable broth into flour. Return this mixture into remaining broth. Stir until sauce thickens.

5. Heat remaining 2 tablespoons butter in a skillet and fry onions and garlic until deep brown. Stir into sauce.

6. Pour sauce over fish and bake for 40 minutes, or until fish flakes easily when tested with a fork.

7. Arrange on a heated platter and serve with sauce spooned over the fish.

Serves 6

baked fillet of flounder, spanish style

6 flounder fillets or other whitefish fillets

Salt and freshly ground pepper

SAUCE

¼ cup butter
1 large onion, chopped
1 green pepper, chopped
1 clove garlic, chopped

¼ cup all-purpose flour
2 cups tomato juice
1½ teaspoons salt
¼ teaspoon pepper

1. Preheat oven to 350° F. (Moderate).

2. Place flounder fillets side by side in a single layer in a greased 9 × 13 × 2-inch baking pan. Sprinkle with salt and pepper to taste.

3. To prepare sauce, melt butter in a saucepan and sauté onion, green pepper and garlic until tender. Stir in flour.

4. Gradually stir in tomato juice, salt and pepper. Cook, stirring, until thick.

5. Spoon sauce evenly over fish fillets. Bake for 40 minutes, or until fish flakes easily when tested with a fork.

6. Arrange fillets on a heated platter and spoon pan juices over fish.

Serves 6

flounder roll-ups with mushroom sauce

6 flounder fillets
Salt and freshly ground
  pepper
1 (12-ounce) can kernel
  corn, drained
1 (1-pound) can sliced
  carrots, drained and
  mashed

¼ cup butter
8 mushrooms, sliced
⅓ cup all-purpose flour
2 cups milk
Paprika (optional)

1. Preheat oven to 350° F. (Moderate).
2. Sprinkle fillets with salt and pepper.
3. Mix corn and carrots. Divid mixture into 6 parts. Spread on fillets and roll up. Place fillets side by side, seam side down, on a greased baking pan.
4. Bake for 35 minutes, or until fish flakes easily when tested with a fork.
5. While the fish is baking, heat butter in a sauce-pan and sauté mushrooms until slightly wilted.
6. Stir in flour. Gradually stir in milk. Cook, stirring, over low heat until sauce bubbles and thickens. Season to taste with salt and pepper.
7. With a pancake turner carefully place fish rolls on a heated platter. Spoon hot sauce over fillets. Sprinkle with paprika.

Serves 6

stuffed flounder or whitefish

12 small flounder fillets OR
  2 large whitefish fillets
Salt
½ cup butter
8 mushrooms, chopped

1 large onion, chopped
1 tomato, chopped
2 tablespoons chopped dill
Juice of 1 lemon
1 teaspoon salt

1. Preheat oven to 350° F. (Moderate).
2. Sprinkle fillets with salt. Place half the fillets in a shallow baking pan side by side.
3. In a skillet melt butter and add remaining ingredients. Simmer until bubbly.
4. With a slotted spoon, spoon vegetable mixture over fillets.
5. Top with remaining fillets. Pour pan juices over fish.
6. Bake for 40 minutes, or until fish flakes easily when tested with a fork. Baste with pan juices several times during baking.
7. Arrange fillets on a heated platter and serve immediately.

Serves 6

baked pompano

6 pompano fillets	tomatoes, drained and chopped
Salt and freshly ground pepper	6 slices American cheese, cut into halves
¼ cup melted butter	Parsley
1 (1-pound) can stewed	

1. Preheat oven to 350° F. (Moderate).
2. Sprinkle fillets with salt and pepper.
3. Place fillets side by side in a single layer in a greased shallow baking pan. Brush with butter. Top with tomatoes and strips of cheese.
4. Bake for 30–35 minutes, or until fish is cooked and cheese is melted.
5. Arrange on a heated platter. Garnish with parsley.

Serves 6

stuffed fillet of sole or gray sole

12 sole fillets

Salt and freshly ground
  pepper

STUFFING
½ cup butter
2 small onions, chopped

1 cup chopped celery
6 cups soft bread crumbs

TOPPING
¼ cup melted butter

¼ cup grated Parmesan
  cheese

1. Preheat oven to 350° F. (Moderate).
2. Sprinkle fillets with salt and pepper.
3. Heat butter in a skillet and sauté onions and celery until golden brown. Stir in bread crumbs. Season with salt and pepper to taste.
4. Place 6 of the fillets in a greased shallow baking pan. Top each fillet with some of the stuffing mixture. Place remaining fillets on top.
5. Brush fillets with melted butter and sprinkle with Parmesan cheese.
6. Bake fillets for 35–40 minutes, or until fish flakes easily when tested with a fork.
7. Arrange fillets on heated platter and serve immediately.

Serves 6

red snapper with hard-boiled egg sauce

1 red snapper, about
  3 pounds
Salt

Freshly ground pepper
Lemon juice

HARD-BOILED EGG SAUCE

⅓ cup butter	4 hard-cooked eggs,
⅓ cup all-purpose flour	chopped
2 cups milk	1 dill pickle, finely chopped

1. Preheat oven to 350° F. (Moderate).

2. Sprinkle snapper inside and out with salt, pepper and lemon juice.

3. Place snapper in a greased shallow baking pan. Bake for 40–45 minutes, or until fish flakes easily when tested with a fork.

4. While snapper is cooking, prepare sauce. In a saucepan melt butter. Stir in flour. Gradually stir in milk.

5. Stir in eggs and pickle. Season to taste with salt and pepper.

6. Serve snapper arranged on a heated platter. Spoon hot egg sauce over the fish.

Serves 6

fried halibut scallops

2 pounds boneless and	1 cup matzoh meal
skinless halibut	Oil
2 eggs	Tartar Sauce (Page 98) and
2 teaspoons salt	lemon wedges (optional)

1. Cut halibut into 1-inch cubes.

2. Beat eggs and salt in a bowl.

3. Dip halibut cubes into egg and then into matzoh meal, coating thoroughly.

4. Fry halibut in hot oil (1 inch deep) until brown on all sides, about 5–6 minutes.

5. Arrange on a heated platter. Serve with tartar sauce and lemon wedges.

Serves 6

fried carp slices

6 slices carp, 1 inch thick
Salt and freshly ground
  pepper
1 egg, well beaten

2 cups matzoh meal
⅓ cup butter
Lemon wedges

1. Sprinkle carp with salt and pepper. Dip slices into beaten egg on both sides. Dredge carp in matzoh meal coating slices completely.
2. Heat butter in a 10-inch skillet. Add carp and fry slowly for 12–15 minutes, or until carp is golden brown on both sides and flakes easily when tested with a fork.
3. Serve on a heated platter with lemon wedges.

Serves 6

boiled fish

1 quart water
½ cup chopped celery
½ cup chopped green
  pepper
½ cup diced carrots
1 large onion, sliced

¼ cup chopped parsley
1 tablespoon salt
1 teaspoon sugar
6 pike, carp, whitefish, or
  salmon fillets

1. In a 10- to 12-inch skillet (depending upon the size of the fish) combine water, vegetables, parsley, salt and sugar. Simmer, covered, for 45 minutes.
2. Add fish fillets. Cover and simmer for another 20 minutes, or until fish is tender.
3. Remove fish with a slotted spoon and serve hot or cold with some of the vegetables from the poaching water.

Serves 6

jellied pickled fish

1 sea bass, about 6 pounds
1 large onion, sliced
3 carrots, sliced
2 tablespoons salt
¼ cup sugar
½ cup white vinegar

1 tablespoon whole pickling
  spice
2 envelopes unflavored
  gelatin
¼ cup water

1. Have sea bass filleted and cut into serving-sized pieces. Reserve the bones and head.
2. In a large saucepan combine bones and fish head, onion, carrots and water to cover. Simmer, covered, for 45 minutes.
3. Strain into another saucepan. Reserve carrot slices.
4. Add fish to strained fish broth.
5. Add salt, sugar, vinegar and pickling spice. Simmer for 30 minutes.
6. Using a pancake turner, carefully remove fish and place in a shallow bowl.
7. Combine gelatin and water and add to fish broth, stirring until dissolved. Strain over fish.
8. Add carrot slices. Chill until firm.

Serves 4–6

sweet and sour cod

4 cod steaks
1 teaspoon salt
1 cup water
⅓ cup white vinegar
1 tablespoon whole pickling
  spice

¼ cup sugar
1 lemon, sliced
1 onion, sliced
1 tomato, sliced
Tartar Sauce (Page 98),
  optional

1. Preheat oven to 350° F. (Moderate).
2. Place cod steaks in a shallow baking pan.

3. In a small bowl mix salt, water, vinegar, pickling spice and sugar. Pour over fish.

4. Top with lemon, onion and tomato slices.

5. Bake for 1 hour, or until fish flakes easily when tested with a fork.

6. Remove fish with slotted spoon, reserving onion and tomato slices to be used as garnish.

7. Serve hot or cold with tartar sauce.

Serves 4

fish cutlets

3 pounds any combination of fresh salmon and halibut	3 potatoes, peeled, diced and cooked
½ cup olive oil	1 large onion, chopped
4 teaspoons salt	2 tablespoons butter
½ teaspoon pepper	4 eggs
1 (1-pound) can salmon, drained and flaked	Oil
	Tomato Sauce (Page 101), optional

1. Preheat oven to 350° F. (Moderate).

2. Cut fresh salmon and halibut into serving pieces and place in a baking pan.

3. Pour oil over fish. Add 2 teaspoons salt and pepper. Bake for 1 hour.

4. Cool. Remove skin and bones. Flake fish into a bowl. Stir in canned salmon.

5. Mash potatoes and add to fish mixture.

6. Sauté onion in butter until golden brown.

7. Add onion, eggs and remaining 2 teaspoons salt to fish and mix well. Shape into 16 patties.

8. Heat ½ inch of oil in a skillet. Brown patties evenly on both sides, turning once. Drain on absorbent paper.

9. Arrange cutlets on a heated platter and serve with tomato sauce.

Serves 8

codfish cakes

2 pounds cod fillets
5 teaspoons salt
1 onion, sliced
4 eggs
½ cup water
¼ cup matzoh meal

½ teaspoon pepper
Oil
Tomato Sauce (Page 101),
    or Hard-Boiled Egg
    Sauce (Page 36),
    optional

1. Place cod in a skillet. Add 2 teaspoons salt, onion and enough water to cover. Cover skillet and simmer for 15–20 minutes, or until cod flakes easily when tested with a fork.
2. Drain and flake cod into a bowl. Stir in remaining salt and ingredients except oil and sauces.
3. Shape into 12 patties.
4. Fry patties in hot oil (½ inch deep) for 5 minutes on each side.
5. Arrange patties on a heated platter and serve with tomato sauce or hard-boiled egg sauce.

Serves 6

steamed halibut, japanese style

3 large halibut steaks, cut
    into halves
2 teaspoons sugar
2 teaspoons salt
½ teaspoon pepper
1 teaspoon cornstarch
½ teaspoon ginger

4 cloves garlic, chopped
4 scallions, sliced
8 medium mushrooms,
    sliced
6 tablespoons oil
2 tablespoons soy sauce
1 cup water

1. Preheat oven to 350° F. (Moderate).
2. Place halibut in a shallow baking pan.
3. In a small bowl mix sugar, salt, pepper, cornstarch and ginger. Sprinkle fish with this mixture.
4. Sprinkle fish with garlic, scallions and mushrooms.

5. Combine oil and soy sauce and pour over fish.

6. Place this pan in a larger pan. Add 1 cup water to larger pan. Cover larger pan loosely with foil. Bake for 1 hour.

7. Arrange fish on a heated platter. Spoon pan juices over halibut and serve immediately.

Serves 6

halibut cantonese

3 large halibut steaks, cut
  into halves
1 clove garlic, minced
Oil
2 cups water
1 small onion, chopped
½ cup chopped celery
2 tablespoons chopped
  parsley

1 tablespoon chopped dill
1 tablespoon sugar
1 tablespoon cornstarch
  mixed with 2 tablespoons
  water
1 teaspoon white vinegar
1 egg white
Salt

1. Place halibut pieces side by side in a shallow baking pan. Sprinkle with garlic. Brush with oil. Let stand for 1 hour.

2. In a saucepan combine water, onion, celery, parsley, dill and sugar. Bring to a boil, lower heat and simmer, covered, for 30 minutes.

3. Strain broth into a saucepan.

4. Stir in cornstarch mixture and vinegar. Cook, stirring, over low heat until thickened.

5. Beat egg white until only half whipped. Stir into hot sauce. Season to taste with salt.

6. Meanwhile, broil fish until lightly browned, about 20–25 minutes, or until fish flakes easily when tested with a fork.

7. Place halibut on a heated serving platter and spoon sauce over fish. Serve immediately.

Serves 6

Vegetable Dishes

Mother could have saved herself a lot of trouble. Instead of screaming at her kids to eat their vegetables because "they're good for you, have minerals and vitamins and will make you strong, so eat them or you'll get a slap," all she had to do was get the recipe for turkey neck.

Turkey neck? All vegetables?

Turkey neck. All vegetables.

And cutlets. And steaks. All vegetables. For Those Who Used To Get Slapped. Disguised by a master chef who keeps getting bids from the CIA. He turned them down because he refused to keep his secrets secret. Now *you've* got them.

Not all vegetables have to wear a mask. When cooking them, the simplest procedures and the fewest additives will enable them to retain all the minerals and vitamins Mama was so concerned about.

We like to serve each vegetable on individual plates so that the natural juices don't run into one another. Makes 'em pretty exclusive.

vegetable cutlets

6 medium potatoes
¼ cup butter
2 onions, chopped
6 mushrooms, chopped
1 (16-ounce) can diced
 carrots, drained
1 (16-ounce) can cut green
 beans, drained

1 (16-ounce) can peas,
 drained
3 eggs
2 cups matzoh meal
 (approximately)
Salt and freshly ground
 pepper
Vegetable Cutlet Gravy
 (Page 44), optional

1. Preheat oven to 350° F. (Moderate).
2. Cook potatoes in boiling salted water 20 minutes, or until tender. Peel and mash.
3. In a skillet heat butter and sauté onions and mushrooms until tender.
4. Pour mushroom mixture into bowl with mashed potatoes. Stir in carrots, green beans, peas and 2 eggs. Blend thoroughly. Add enough matzoh meal so that mixture can be shaped into large patties. Season to taste with salt and pepper.
5. Shape into 12 patties. Beat well the 1 remaining egg. Brush patties on both sides, coating thoroughly. Place on a greased cookie sheet.
6. Bake for 45 minutes, or until lightly browned.
7. Serve hot topped with Vegetable Cutlet Gravy.

Serves 6–8

vegetable cutlet gravy

4 tablespoons butter
1 onion, chopped
1 carrot, diced
1 cup chopped celery
1 green pepper, chopped
1 clove garlic, chopped
1 (1-pound) can tomatoes,
    undrained

3 cups Mushroom Water
    (Page 100)
1 tablespoon mushroom
    powder
¼ cup all-purpose flour
Salt and freshly ground
    pepper to taste
Paprika

1. In a saucepan heat 2 tablespoons butter and sauté onion, carrot, celery, green pepper and garlic until soft, about 5 minutes.

2. Add tomatoes, mushroom water and mushroom powder. Simmer for 20 minutes.

3. Mix remaining 2 tablespoons butter and flour and enough water to make a paste. Stir into saucepan and cook until sauce bubbles and thickens.

4. Season to taste with salt, pepper and paprika.

5. Serve hot spooned over Vegetable Cutlets (Page 43).

Enough for 6 servings

fricassee balls with gravy

FRICASSEE BALLS
12 mushrooms
1 green pepper
1 carrot
1 onion
2 stalks celery

1 clove garlic
¼ cup butter
4 eggs
2 cups matzoh meal (ap-
    proximately)

GRAVY

4 cups Mushroom Water
(Page 100)
1 onion
2 stalks celery
1 green pepper
1 clove garlic

1 tomato
1 cup chopped cooked
mushrooms
1 tablespoon salt
¼ teaspoon pepper

1. Grind mushrooms, green pepper, carrot, onion, celery and garlic. If grinder is not available, chop very finely.

2. Heat butter in a skillet. Add vegetables and sauté until mushy. Cool to lukewarm.

3. Stir in eggs and enough matzoh meal to make a mixture thick enough to shape into balls the size of golf balls. Use wet hands to shape balls.

4. To prepare gravy, pour mushroom water into a large Dutch oven.

5. Finely chop or grind onion, celery, green pepper, garlic, tomato and mushrooms. Add this mixture to mushroom water along with the salt and pepper.

6. Bring to a boil, lower heat and simmer for 30 minutes.

7. Add fricassee balls to gravy and simmer, covered, for 30 minutes longer.

8. Serve hot.

Serves 6–8

goulash

1 recipe Fricassee Balls
(Page 44), cooked in
simmering salted water
1 recipe Vegetable Cutlet
Gravy (Page 44)
6 small whole white onions,
cooked

6 carrots, cut in 1-inch
pieces, cooked
2 cups 1-inch pieces celery,
cooked
1 cup cooked peas
2 tablespoons butter
1 green pepper, chopped

1. Prepare fricassee balls as directed.
2. Prepare vegetable cutlet gravy as directed in a large saucepan.
3. Add cooked vegetables to gravy.
4. In a skillet heat butter and sauté green pepper until wilted. Stir into gravy.
5. Drain fricassee balls and add to gravy. Heat until bubbly.
6. Serve in large heated bowls like stew.

Serves 6

stuffed green peppers with sauce

SAUCE
1 (1-pound 12-ounce) can
  tomato purée
1½ cups water
½ cup sugar (an additional
  ½ cup sugar may be
  added if a sweeter sauce
  is desired)

1½ tablespoons salt
1 apple, peeled, cored and
  grated
1 teaspoon sour salt

PEPPERS
6 green peppers
½ cup butter
2 large onions, chopped
2 cups (1 pound) brown
  rice, cooked and drained

2 eggs
1 tablespoon salt
¼ teaspoon pepper

1. To prepare sauce, combine all ingredients in a saucepan and simmer for 30 minutes.
2. Preheat oven to 350° F. (Moderate).
3. While sauce is simmering prepare the peppers. Slice tops from green peppers and remove seeds. Cook peppers in boiling salted water for 5 minutes. Drain.
4. In a skillet heat butter and sauté onions until transparent.

cheese filling

2 pounds farmer cheese
2 egg yolks
¼ cup melted butter
¼ cup matzoh meal

¼ cup sugar if a sweeter
pirogen is desired
(optional)

1. In a bowl combine all ingredients.
2. Chill until ready to use.
3. Use as filling for pirogen dough.
Filling for 50 small pirogen

potato filling

¼ cup butter
3 cups chopped onion
4 cups cooked mashed
Idaho potatoes

Salt and freshly ground
pepper

1. In a skillet heat butter and sauté onion until golden brown.
2. Stir in mashed potatoes, salt and pepper to taste.
3. Cool.
4. Use as filling for pirogen dough or knishes.
Filling for 50 small pirogen or two 12-inch knishes

blueberry filling

2 pints fresh blueberries   ½ cup sugar

1. Combine blueberries and sugar in a bowl and blend thoroughly.
2. Use as filling for pirogen dough.
Filling for 50 small pirogen

apricot filling

25 fresh apricots, pitted   ½ cup sugar
    and diced

1. Combine apricots and sugar in a bowl and blend thoroughly.
2. Use as filling for pirogen dough.

Filling for 50 small pirogen

cherry filling

2 pounds dark sweet   ⅓ cup sugar
    cherries, pitted and
    halved

1. Combine cherries and sugar in a bowl and blend thoroughly.
2. Use as filling for pirogen dough.

Filling for 50 small pirogen

kashe varnishkes

2 large onions, chopped   1 Basic Kashe recipe
¼ cup oil   (Page 52)
2 cups uncooked bow ties   Salt
    (noodles)

1. In a skillet, sauté onions in oil until golden brown.
2. Cook bow ties in boiling salted water according to package directions. Drain.
3. Stir noodles and kashe into onions and reheat. Season to taste with salt.

Serves 6

variation

Spoon kashe varnishkes into serving dish. Cover with Stewed Mushrooms (Page 60) and serve immediately.

baked macaroni and cheese

2 cups uncooked elbow
   macaroni
½ cup butter
½ cup all-purpose flour
1½ cups milk

1½ cups sour cream
1 tablespoon salt
½ tablespoon pepper
1 (10-ounce) bar mild
   Cheddar cheese, grated

1. Preheat oven to 350° F. (Moderate).
2. Cook macaroni in boiling salted water according to package directions. Drain and rinse with cold water. Pour into a 3-quart casserole.
3. In a saucepan melt butter and stir in flour. Gradually stir in milk and sour cream. Add salt and pepper.
4. Cook over low heat, stirring constantly, until sauce bubbles and thickens.
5. Reserve 1 cup grated cheese for the top of the casserole. Toss macaroni with remaining cheese.
6. Pour sauce over macaroni and mix thoroughly. Sprinkle with reserved cheese.
7. Bake for 1 hour, or until bubbly and brown.
8. Serve immediately.

Serves 6

potato pancakes

6 potatoes
1 onion
2 eggs, well beaten
1½ teaspoons salt

½ cup all-purpose flour
Oil
Sour cream or applesauce
   (optional)

1. Peel potatoes and grate finely into a bowl of cold water. (This removes excess starch and makes potatoes stiff rather than soggy.)

2. In another bowl grate onion finely. Mix with eggs, salt and flour.

3. Drain potatoes and press out all liquid.

4. Stir potatoes into batter and mix well.

5. Heat ½ inch oil in a 10-inch skillet. Drop batter by tablespoons into hot oil.

6. Flatten out to 4-inch pancakes and fry slowly until very brown and crisp. Turn and brown on the other side.

7. Arrange on a heated platter. Serve with sour cream or applesauce.

Serves 6

variation

Special French Fries: Cut slightly browned, cooked potato pancakes into strips. Drop a few at a time into deep oil heated to 360° F. and fry until brown and crisp.

NOTE: Leftover pancakes can be used in this manner.

cheese pancakes

1½ pounds pot cheese
½ teaspoon salt
6 eggs, well beaten
½ cup all-purpose flour

Butter
Confectioners' sugar and
   jam (optional)

1. Combine pot cheese, salt, eggs and flour and beat until smooth.

2. In a skillet melt butter to a depth of ¼ inch. Spoon batter into skillet shaping pancakes into 3½-

inch rounds (if the pancakes are any larger, they will be difficult to turn).

3. Brown evenly on both sides, turning once.

4. Arrange on heated plates and sprinkle with confectioners' sugar or serve with jam.

Serves 4–6

matzoh meal pancakes

4 eggs, well beaten	½ teaspoon salt
¼ cup melted butter	Butter
1 cup matzoh meal	Applesauce or sour cream
½ cup water	(optional)

1. Combine first 5 ingredients and beat until smooth.

2. In a skillet heat butter to a depth of ¼ inch.

3. Drop batter by tablespoons into skillet and brown evenly on both sides, turning once.

4. Serve hot topped with applesauce or sour cream.

Ten 4-inch pancakes

fried matzohs

8 matzohs	3 tablespoons butter
½ teaspoon salt	Jam, applesauce or sour
¼ teaspoon pepper	cream (optional)
5 eggs, well beaten	

1. Soak matzohs in lukewarm water until soft. Drain thoroughly. Matzohs will be crumbly.

2. Season with salt and pepper. Pour eggs over matzohs and mix thoroughly.

3. Heat butter in a 12-inch skillet. Add matzoh mixture and let it set for a minute or two. Then stir with a fork until matzoh is dry and lightly browned.

4. Serve hot with jam, applesauce or sour cream.

Serves 4

matzoh brei

3 matzohs
½ teaspoon salt
¼ teaspoon pepper
2 eggs, well beaten

2 tablespoons butter
Jam, applesauce or sour
　cream (optional)

1. Soak matzohs in lukewarm water until soft. Drain thoroughly. Matzohs will be crumbly.
2. Season with salt and pepper. Stir in eggs.
3. Heat butter in an 8-inch skillet. Add matzoh mixture and cook without stirring. Brown on one side, turn carefully with 2 pancake turners and brown on the other side.
4. Serve hot with jam, applesauce or sour cream.

Serves 2

french toast

2 eggs
1 cup milk
4 thick slices Challah
　(Page 106)

Butter
Maple syrup, jam or jelly
　(optional)

1. Beat eggs and milk together.
2. Dip challah slices into egg mixture to coat thoroughly.
3. In a skillet melt butter to a depth of ¼ inch. Add challah and brown evenly on both sides, turning once.
4. Serve hot with maple syrup or a favorite jam or jelly.

Serves 4

marmaliga

2 cups water
2 cups milk
1 teaspoon salt
1 cup yellow cornmeal
¼ cup butter

Cottage cheese (optional)
Sour cream (optional)
Grated Parmesan cheese
(optional)

1. In a saucepan combine first five ingredients.
2. Bring to a boil, stirring constantly, and cook until butter is melted and mixture is thick, about 15–20 minutes.
3. Serve topped with a spoonful of cottage cheese and sour cream. (Marmaliga can also be served plain or sprinkled wth grated Parmesan cheese.)

Serves 6

vegetables with sour cream

¾ cup sour cream
1 cup chopped mixed
vegetables*

Salt and freshly ground
pepper

1. In a bowl mix sour cream and vegetables.
2. Season to taste with salt and pepper. Serve cold.

1 serving

Scallions, cucumbers, tomatoes, grated carrots, celery, raw cauliflower, raw chopped spinach, cooked shredded beets, grated radishes, raw white turnips or shredded lettuce.

cream dishes

¾ cup sour cream OR
½ cup heavy cream

Granulated or brown sugar
(optional)

1. Mix sour cream or heavy cream with any of the following, either alone or in combination:
- 1 banana, sliced
- 2 cling peach halves, diced
- 1 cup blueberries
- 1 cup sliced, hulled strawberries
- 1 cup pitted dark sweet cherries
- ½ cup canned drained figs
- ½ cup cooked pitted prunes
- ½ cup well-drained crushed pineapple

2. Sprinkle top of dish with granulated or brown sugar.
3. Serve very cold.

1 serving

sour milk

1 heaping tablespoon sour cream	8 ounces milk Fresh fruit (optional)

1. Spoon sour cream into an empty glass. Pour in milk and combine, mixing well.
2. Set glass in a warm place (the back of your stove is a good place) and let stand, uncovered, for 48 hours.
3. When mixture has become firm, cover and refrigerate.
4. Serve when thoroughly chilled. Sour milk is eaten with a spoon.
5. Sour milk may be eaten with fresh fruit as you would yoghurt.

1 serving

Eggs and Omelets

If Ratner's soups have emerged as headliners, then eggs are their unheralded supporting players. And like all great supporting players, their primary claim to fame is versatility. Eggs can be boiled, poached, baked, fried, scrambled, shirred, made into omelets or combined with other ingredients as part of an interesting and provocative dish. Their versatility includes nutritional value (protein, iron, Vitamins A and D) and economy —low purchase cost and an ability to subjugate their personality into leftovers.

But beware, homemakers! Abe, omelet chef extraordinaire, cautions that the art is not in the egg—but in the pan!

An omelet pan is never washed. After the eggs are removed the pan must be wiped (repeat—wiped, never washed) clean, salted, swished with hot oil, wiped clean again and returned to its place. Keep it up front. Chances are you'll be using it again very quickly.

boiled eggs

1. Place eggs in cold water. Add salt and bring to a boil. Reduce heat and simmer for 3 minutes for soft,

6 minutes for medium and 12–15 minutes for hard cooked.

2. Soft-cooked eggs should be rinsed in cold water to stop cooking and served at once with salt and pepper and a bit of butter, if desired.

3. The hard-cooked eggs should cool in the cooking water and then should be drained and covered with cold water. Roll egg on hard surface to crack shell all over. Peel. Use as desired or store, covered, in the refrigerator.

poached eggs

½ teaspoon salt   Salt and freshly ground
2 eggs   pepper
Buttered toast

1. Fill a saucepan with water to the depth of 2 inches. Bring to a boil, lower heat and simmer. Stir in ½ teaspoon salt.

2. Break 1 egg into a bowl and then slide the egg into simmering water. Repeat using second egg.

3. Simmer for 3–5 minutes, depending on the firmness desired.

4. Remove eggs with a slotted spoon. Place eggs on buttered toast and sprinkle with salt and pepper to taste.

1 serving

poached eggs on spinach
(eggs florentine)

¾ cup Creamed Spinach   Salt and freshly ground
   (Page 65)   pepper
2 Poached Eggs (see above)   Grated Parmesan cheese
                                      (optional)

1. Prepare creamed spinach as directed. When hot spoon into a shallow casserole.

2. Prepare poached eggs as directed and place on top of creamed spinach. Sprinkle with salt and pepper to taste.

3. Serve immediately or sprinkle with grated cheese and run under the broiler until cheese melts.

1 serving

basic scrambled eggs

2 eggs
1 tablespoon butter

Salt and freshly ground
    pepper

1. Beat eggs in a small bowl.

2. In a small skillet heat butter. Pour eggs into skillet.

3. Stir eggs gently while cooking until eggs are set but tender and moist.

4. Season to taste with salt and pepper.

1 serving

variations

1. *Onion:* Add 3 tablespoons finely chopped onion to butter in skillet. Sauté until golden. Add eggs and cook as directed above.

2. *Mushroom:* Add 3 tablespoons chopped fresh mushrooms to butter in skillet. Sauté for 1 minute. Add eggs and cook as directed above.

3. *Mushroom and Onions:* Add 2 tablespoons chopped fresh mushrooms and 1 tablespoon chopped onion to butter in skillet. Sauté until golden. Add eggs and cook as directed above.

4. *Smoked Salmon:* Scramble eggs as above. When

eggs are half cooked, stir in 3 tablespoons diced smoked salmon. Continue cooking as directed above.

5. *Smoked Salmon and Onions:* Add 2 tablespoons chopped onion to butter in skillet. Sauté until golden. Add eggs and cook until eggs are half cooked. Stir in 2 tablespoons diced smoked salmon. Continue cooking as directed above.

basic french omelet

2 eggs
2 tablespoons milk or water
½ teaspoon salt

Dash of pepper
1 tablespoon butter

1. In a bowl beat eggs, milk, salt and pepper until just blended.
2. In a small skillet heat butter.
3. When butter sizzles, pour in egg mixture and cook over moderate heat without stirring until eggs are set.
4. Lift edges of omelet and allow uncooked eggs to run underneath. Cook until top is set but still moist.
5. With a spatula lift one side of the omelet and fold in half in pan.
6. Slide omelet out onto a plate and serve immediately.

1 serving

variations

1. *Cheese:* Shred or grate ½ cup American, Cheddar or Swiss cheese. Sprinkle cheese over omelet just before it is folded.
2. *Fresh Tomato:* In a separate skillet sauté 1 small tomato, chopped, in 1 tablespoon butter until mushy. Season to taste with salt. Spoon over omelet just before it is folded.

3. *Western:* Beat eggs as above. Stir in 1 tablespoon chopped onion, 1 tablespoon chopped green pepper, 1 tablespoon crumbled protose or textured vegetable protein. Prepare omelet as directed above.

4. *Spinach:* Beat eggs. Stir in 3 tablespoons finely chopped cooked spinach. Prepare omelet as directed above.

5. *Sautéed Mushroom:* In a separate skillet heat 1 tablespoon butter and sauté 3 mushrooms, sliced, until tender. Spoon mushrooms over omelet before folding.

6. *Asparagus:* Beat eggs. Fold in ¼ cup 1-inch pieces drained, cooked or canned asparagus. Prepare omelet as directed above.

7. *Spanish Omelet:* See recipe for Spanish Sauce (Page 101). Prepare omelet as directed and slide onto a plate. Top omelet with ½ cup of the Spanish Sauce heated until piping hot.

puffy omelet

6 eggs, separated
1 tablespoon flour
1 teaspoon salt
⅓ cup milk

¼ cup Clarified Butter
(Page 96)
Jam or jelly (optional)

1. In a bowl beat egg whites until stiff but not dry.

2. Using the same beater, beat egg yolks, flour, salt and milk in a small bowl.

3. Pour egg yolk mixture over egg whites and fold together until light and well blended.

4. Heat butter in a 10-inch skillet until it sizzles. Pour in egg mixture. Cook without stirring until brown on under side.

5. Place pan under broiler and broil until top of omelet is golden brown. Quickly fold omelet with a spatula and turn out onto a heated platter.

6. Serve omelet topped with your favorite jam or jelly.

Serves 4

shirred eggs*

2 eggs   1 tablespoon butter
Salt and freshly ground
  pepper

1. Preheat oven to 350° F. (Moderate).
2. Grease a shallow individual casserole or ramekin and drop in 2 eggs. Sprinkle with salt and pepper to taste.
3. Dot egg yolks with butter.
4. Bake for 15–20 minutes, or until whites are set and yolks are still soft.

1 serving

---

* *Shirred Eggs can be sprinkled heavily with grated American or Parmesan cheese and baked as above.*

Salads

Salads are to chefs as landscapes are to painters; to be used as background, part of the scene, or to stand alone. Salads provide color to a meal as well as nutrition. Like paints, their ingredients can be mixed to achieve a desired result and, lest we neglect the sculptor, they can be shaped, sliced, slivered, cubed, rolled or curled.

Crispness and freshness are the keys to salads no matter how they are used. Greens should be thoroughly washed and then shaken. Follow through by wrapping the greens in paper towelling to remove any residual traces of moisture. Since salad ingredients quickly become limp, place them in the refrigerator immediately after washing. Salads, to retain their freshness, should be dressed prior to serving.

At Ratner's they have spent a professional lifetime creating new and different salad combinations. The results have been both satisfying and attractive to the clientele. But take heart, dear novice! All it requires is a little experience and a lot of imagination. There are no complexities involved, no special tools required.

Imagination working?

Go!

tossed salad

1 small head red cabbage,
  shredded
1 head iceberg lettuce,
  broken into bite-sized
  pieces

2 carrots, shredded
1 cup French Dressing
  (Page 97) or Russian
  Dressing (Page 98)

1. In a bowl combine all ingredients except dressing. Cover and chill.
2. When ready to serve, pour French or Russian dressing over the salad and toss to blend thoroughly.

Serves 6

potato salad

3 pounds Idaho potatoes
1 onion, finely chopped
1 carrot, grated
2 tablespoons chopped
  parsley
1 tablespoon chopped dill
2 tablespoons vinegar

1½ teaspoons salt
½ teaspoon pepper
½ teaspoon dry mustard
1 cup Blender Mayonnaise
  (Page 97)
1 cup sour cream
1 teaspoon sugar

1. Cook potatoes in boiling salted water to cover, about 30 minutes, until tender. Cool. Peel and dice.
2. In a large bowl combine potatoes, onion, carrot, parsley and dill.
3. Mix together remaining ingredients and add to potatoes. Toss until well blended. Correct seasonings.
4. Chill until ready to serve.

Serves 6–8

german potato salad

¼ cup butter
2 large onions, chopped
3 pounds new potatoes,
  cooked, peeled and sliced
1 cup chopped celery
2 dill pickles, chopped

¼ cup capers, drained
1⅓ cups French Dressing
  (Page 97)
4 hard-cooked eggs,
  chopped

1. In a 10-inch skillet heat butter and sauté onions until golden brown.
2. Stir in remaining ingredients and heat until salad is warm.
3. This potato salad may also be served cold, if desired.

Serves 6

coleslaw

1 medium head green
  cabbage
1 onion, chopped
1 green pepper, chopped
1 carrot, shredded
½ teaspoon pepper

1 tablespoon salt
½ cup white vinegar
⅔ cup water
2 tablespoons sugar
1½ cups Blender Mayon-
  naise (Page 97)

1. Remove outside leaves of cabbage and discard. Cut cabbage into quarters, removing hard cores. Shred.
2. Add all remaining ingredients except mayonnaise to the cabbage. Let stand for 2 hours and then drain thoroughly.
3. Stir in mayonnaise and chill until ready to use.

Serves 6–8

macaroni salad

2 cups elbow macaroni,
  cooked and drained
1 cup chopped celery
2 scallions, chopped
2 carrots, shredded

1 (4-ounce) jar pimientos,
  chopped
1 cup Blender Mayonnaise
  (Page 97)
Salt and freshly ground
  pepper to taste

1. In a bowl combine all ingredients and toss until
well blended.
2. Chill until ready to serve.

Serves 6

tuna salad

2 (7-ounce) cans tuna,
  packed in water
2 cups chopped celery
½ cup Blender Mayonnaise
  (Page 97)

Salt and freshly ground
  pepper to taste
Lettuce
Green pepper rings
Sliced tomatoes

1. Combine first 4 ingredients and blend thoroughly.
2. Chill until ready to serve.
3. Serve in a mound on lettuce leaves or shredded
lettuce garnished with green pepper rings and sliced
tomatoes.

Serves 6

pickled beets

2 (1-pound) cans sliced
  beets, undrained
1 red onion, sliced
1 teaspoon salt

2 tablespoons whole
  pickling spice
1 cup white vinegar
¼ cup sugar

1. In a glass or earthenware bowl, combine all ingredients.
2. Chill for several hours.
3. Drain.
4. Serve on lettuce leaves or plain as a relish.

Serves 6–8

pickled beets and cucumbers

1 recipe Pickled Beets
(Page 88)

1 large cucumber, peeled
and sliced

1. Prepare beets as directed, adding cucumber.

Serves 8

spring salad

2 cucumbers, chopped
1 bunch radishes, chopped
2 scallions, chopped

Salt and freshly ground
pepper
1 pound cottage cheese
1 cup sour cream

1. Mix vegetables with salt and pepper to taste.
2. Place vegetables in a shallow salad bowl and refrigerate until ready to use. Drain.
3. Place cottage cheese on top and spoon sour cream over all.
4. Serve immediately.

Serves 6

winter fruit salad

2 oranges, sectioned
1 grapefruit, sectioned
2 apples, diced
2 pears, diced
2 bananas, sliced
1 cup black grapes, stemmed

1 cup cider
2 tablespoons lemon juice
Lettuce
1½ cups Blender Mayonnaise (Page 97)

1. In a bowl mix fruits with cider and lemon juice. Chill for several hours.
2. Drain and reserve juice.* Arrange fruits on lettuce leaves.
3. Serve with mayonnaise diluted with about ⅓ cup of the fruit juice.

Serves 6

———
* *This juice may be used for drinks or as a base for punch.*

summer fruit salad

1 cup diced cantaloupe
1 cup diced pineapple
1 navel orange, sectioned
1 grapefruit, sectioned
1 cup whole strawberries
1 cup blueberries
1 cup stemmed, seedless green grapes

1 cup diced watermelon or other melon
1 cup orange juice
1 cup pineapple juice
1 tablespoon lemon juice
½ cup Blender Mayonnaise (Page 97) and ½ cup sour cream (optional)

1. In a bowl mix all fruits and juices. Chill for several hours.
2. Drain* and serve on lettuce leaves.
3. Dress with mayonnaise mixed with sour cream.

Serves 6

———
* *This juice may be used for drinks or as a base for punch.*

waldorf salad

4 apples, cored and diced
1 tablespoon lemon juice
1 cup chopped celery
½ cup raisins
1 cup chopped walnuts

½ cup Blender Mayon-
naise (Page 97)
½ cup sour cream
Lettuce

1. Combine all ingredients, except lettuce, and toss to blend well.
2. Chill until ready to serve.
3. Serve spooned on lettuce leaves.

Serves 6

california fruit salad

1 kadota fig
1 slice pineapple
2 large pitted prunes,
cooked
½ cup cubed strawberry
jello

½ cup cottage cheese
2 peach halves
¼ cup Blender Mayon-
naise (Page 97)
1 tablespoon pineapple
juice (optional)

1. Arrange all ingredients except mayonnaise on a bed of lettuce.
2. Serve with mayonnaise mixed with pineapple juice.
1 serving

ratner's special salad

2 peach halves (canned or
fresh)
2 pear halves (canned or
fresh)
1 slice pineapple (canned
or fresh)
2 cooked pitted prunes

1 kadota fig
½ cup cubed strawberry
jello
¼ cup Blender Mayonnaise
(Page 97)
1 tablespoon orange juice
(optional)

1. If fresh fruit is used, peel, halve and remove pit or core. Brush peaches and pears with lemon juice to prevent discoloration.

2. Arrange fruits and jello on a bed of lettuce.

3. Serve with mayonnaise mixed with orange juice.

1 serving

SALAD COMBINATIONS

chopped herring with potato salad

1. Line a salad plate with lettuce leaves or shredded lettuce. Top with a mound of Chopped Herring (Page 3).

2. Garnish with sliced tomatoes, cucumbers and scallions.

3. Serve with Egg Bagels (Page 105) and butter or cream cheese.

tuna salad with potato salad

1. Line a salad plate with lettuce leaves or shredded lettuce. Drain thoroughly a 7-ounce can of tuna fish* and invert onto lettuce in one piece. Top with Blender Mayonnaise (Page 97) or lemon wedges. Add a mound of Potato Salad (Page 86).

2. Garnish with raw carrot sticks, celery hearts or slices of hard-cooked egg.

3. Serve with Cheese Bread (Page 112) and butter.

---

* *This salad combination can also be made by substituting Tuna Salad (Page 88) for the can of tuna.*

macaroni or spring salad
with matjes herring

1. Line a salad plate with lettuce leaves or shredded lettuce. Top with Macaroni Salad (Page 88) or Spring Salad (Page 89) and 1 or 2 matjes herring fillets, well drained and cut into bite-sized pieces.
2. Garnish with sour cream, cucumber slices, tomato wedges and pickle slices.
3. Serve with Crusty Bread (Page 111) and butter.

vegetable liver salad
with potato salad

1. Line a salad plate with lettuce leaves or shredded lettuce. Top with a mound of Chopped Liver (Page 6) and Potato Salad (Page 86).
2. Garnish with radishes and sliced tomatoes.
3. Serve with Rye Bread (Page 108) and butter.

salmon salad and potato salad

1. Line a salad plate with lettuce leaves or shredded lettuce. Top with a small piece of Poached Fish (Salmon) (Page 37)* and a mound of Potato Salad (Page 86).
2. Garnish with lemon wedges, cucumber slices and onion rings.
3. Serve with Challah (Page 106) and butter.

---

* *This salad combination can also be made by substituting Chopped Salmon and Celery (Page 9) for Poached Fish (Salmon).*

egg salad with potato salad

1. Line a salad plate with lettuce leaves or shredded lettuce. Top with 1 or 2 sliced hard-cooked eggs* and a mound of Potato Salad (Page 86).
2. Garnish with white horseradish, celery hearts, a few olives and cherry tomatoes.
3. Serve with Pumpernickel Bread (Page 109) and butter.

This salad combination can also be made by substituting Chopped Eggs and Onions (Page 7) for hard-cooked eggs.

sardine salad with potato salad

1. Line a salad plate witth lettuce leaves or shredded lettuce. Top with well-drained skinless and boneless sardines* and a mound of Potato Salad (Page 86).
2. Garnish with lemon wedges, sliced hard-cooked egg, cucumber and tomato slices.
3. Serve with Whole-Wheat Bread (Page 110) and butter.

This salad combination can also be made by substituting well-drained tomato herring for the sardines.

smoked whitefish with potato salad

1. Line a salad plate with lettuce leaves or shredded lettuce. Top with a section of smoked whitefish* and a

---

This salad combination can also be made by substituting a piece of smoked sable for the whitefish.

mound of Potato Salad (Page 86) and/or a mound of Coleslaw (Page 87).

2. Garnish with lemon wedges, carrot slices, cucumber slices and radishes.

3. Serve with Onion Rolls (Page 102) and butter.

boiled carp salad

1. Line a salad plate with lettuce leaves or shredded lettuce. Top with a section of Boiled Fish (Carp) (Page 37) and a mound of Potato Salad (Page 86) and/or a mound of Coleslaw (Page 87).

2. Garnish with lemon wedges or tartar sauce and tomato slices.

3. Serve with slices of Crusty Bread (Page 111) and butter.

Sauces and Dressings

Only in a democracy like Ratner's can one wallow in the spices of life in all languages. We have Russian dressing, French dressing, English mustard and Spanish sauce. For the nationless we serve mayonnaise, horseradish and tomato sauce.

Most of these sauces and dressings are available at your supermarket in packaged form. So why bother to make them? Because it's no bother to make them. Homemade, they're adjustable to your own taste, more economical and a great way to show off when you're having a dinner party. It's a sure bet someone will say, "Who makes her own sauces and dressings in this day and age?"

Answer: RATNER'S.

And you.

clarified butter

1 pound butter or parve
  margarine

1. Melt butter in a saucepan over low heat. Remove from heat and let stand for 2 minutes.

2. Skim foam from butter, if any, and then pour off clear, oily looking butter into a container.

3. Stop pouring when you reach the milky residue in bottom of pan. Refrigerate until needed.

1⅔ cups

french dressing

1 cup soya oil
⅓ cup red wine vinegar
1 teaspoon sugar

1 clove garlic, chopped
1 teaspoons salt
½ teaspoon pepper

1. Mix all ingredients together in a tightly covered jar and shake well.

2. Keep at room temperature until ready to serve. Shake again before using.

1⅓ cups

blender mayonnaise

Juice of 1 small lemon
4 eggs yolks
Pinch of dry mustard

½ teaspoon salt
1 cup oil

1. In a blender beat together lemon juice, egg yolks and seasonings.

2. Add the oil slowly, one drop at a time, beating all the while until the mayonnaise is thick.

3. Chill until ready to serve.

4. Store in refrigerator for up to 2 weeks.

1½ cups

russian dressing

1 cup Blender Mayonnaise
(Page 97)
2 tablespoons catsup
Few drops of Tabasco
sauce
½ teaspoon salt

1 tablespoon vinegar
1 teaspoon Worcestershire
sauce
1 teaspoon sugar
1 teaspoon paprika
¼ cup water

1. Combine all ingredients in a bowl and blend thoroughly. Dressing should be slightly thickened. Taste should be on the sharp side.
2. Chill until ready to serve.
3. Store in refrigerator for up to 2 weeks.

1½ cups

rosy dressing

1 cup Blender Mayonnaise
(Page 97)

½ cup catsup
2 tablespoons white vinegar

1. Combine all ingredients in a bowl and blend thoroughly.
2. Chill until ready to use.
3. Store in refrigerator for up to 2 weeks.

1⅔ cups

tartar sauce

1 cup Blender Mayonnaise
(Page 97)
¼ cup pickle relish
2 tablespoons finely chopped
onion

2 tablespoons chopped
parsley
2 tablespoons drained
capers (optional)

1. In a small bowl combine all ingredients and blend thoroughly.

2. Chill until ready for use.

NOTE: If desired, tartar sauce may be further flavored with prepared mustard or lemon juice to taste.

1½ cups

horseradish

1 horseradish root, approximately 1 pound
1 cup white vinegar

½ cup sugar
1 beet, canned or freshly
   cooked* (optional)

1. Pare horseradish. Grate finely.

2. Add vinegar and sugar. Mix well. Chill.

About 2 cups

---

* If red horseradish is desired, grate cooked beet and combine with the above before chilling.

english mustard

½ cup dry mustard
1 tablespoon sour cream

½ cup water (approxi-
   mately)
Salt

1. Combine mustard and sour cream and blend thoroughly.

2. Add enough water to achieve desired consistency. Season to taste with salt.

3. Serve as an accompaniment to Egg Roll (Page 49).

⅔ cup

mushroom water

2 pounds mushrooms,   1 quart water
  chopped

1. In a large saucepan combine mushrooms and water. Simmer for 10–15 minutes, or until mushrooms are tender.
2. Strain broth and chill until ready to use. (Remaining chopped mushrooms may also be chilled until ready to use in any dish.)

4 cups

fruit sauce

1 (1-pound 4-ounce) can   pineapple chunks,
  pie-sliced apples,   undrained
  undrained   2 tablespoons cornstarch
½ cup sugar   ¼ cup water
1 (1-pound 1-ounce) can   1 (11-ounce) can mandarin
  pears, drained and diced   oranges, drained
1 (1-pound 4-ounce) can

1. In a saucepan mix apples, sugar, pears and pineapple chunks. Heat until bubbly.
2. Mix cornstarch with water. Stir into fruit. Cook, stirring, over low heat until mixture bubbles and thickens.
3. Stir in mandarin oranges.
4. Keep warm until ready to serve.
5. May be stored in refrigerator for 1 week.

About 7 cups

tomato sauce

(This is a very versatile tomato sauce and can be used for eggs, omelets, codfish cakes, spaghetti, rice, noodles or mashed potatoes.)

2 cups tomato purée	1 tablespoon salt
2 cups water	¼ teaspoon pepper
2 tablespoons sugar	½ teaspoon oregano

1. Combine all ingredients in a large saucepan.
2. Cover and simmer gently for 1 hour.
3. Correct seasonings.

NOTE: This sauce will keep for 2 weeks, if refrigerated.

2 cups

spanish sauce

1 (1-pound 12-ounce) can tomatoes, chopped and undrained	1 cup chopped celery
	½ cup chopped green pepper
1 cup tomato purée	½ cup chopped onion
2 tablespoons butter	½ cup diced carrots
3 cups water	Salt and freshly ground pepper
3 tablespoons sugar	

1. Combine all ingredients except the salt and pepper. Simmer, uncovered, for 1 hour, or until thick.
2. Season to taste.

NOTE: This sauce will keep for 2 weeks, if refrigerated.

1 quart

Breads and Rolls

Winner and still undisputed champion at Ratner's is its famous onion roll, featured on every table with every meal. More than fifteen hundred rolls are baked daily, three thousand on Sunday. And very few live long enough to grow stale. Even to a baker, that's a lotta dough.

Ratner's, in the heart of the metropolis, can still evoke images of Grandma in her kitchen indulging in the time-honored art of baking bread. Result? Diners travel long distances for "Just coffee and a roll." At times they manage a little home-baked challah for dessert.

The Ratner's cookbook offers you these tasty recipes, recommending all unequivocally. But the onion rolls? Well, you've got to stay with the champ.

We dare you to eat just *one*.

onion rolls

DOUGH

1 package active dry yeast
1 cup lukewarm water
2 tablespoons sugar
1½ teaspoons salt

¾ cup whole eggs (about 3)
6 tablespoons oil
4–5 cups all-purpose flour
1 egg, well beaten, for wash

FILLING

1 cup finely chopped onion	1½ teaspoons caraway
1 teaspoon salt	seeds
1 tablespoon poppy seeds	1 cup dry bread crumbs
	¼ cup oil

1. In a bowl soften yeast in lukewarm water. Stir in sugar, salt, eggs, oil and enough flour to form a stiff dough.

2. Knead on a floured surface until smooth and elastic, about 5 minutes. Place dough in a greased bowl and turn to grease top. Let rise, covered, in a warm dry place until doubled in bulk, about 1 hour.

3. Punch down and knead on a floured surface and roll dough into an 18 × 24-inch oblong. Cut dough into twelve 6 × 3-inch pieces.

4. To prepare filling, mix all ingredients in a bowl. Spoon three-fourths of the mixture over dough. Fold one-third of the dough over onions and fold one-third over again from the other side.

5. Place rolls, seam side down, on a greased cookie sheet. Flatten rolls until they are five inches long. Cut rolls in half.

6. Brush rolls with egg wash and sprinkle with remaining onion mixture.* Let rise, covered, in a warm place until doubled in bulk, about 30 minutes.

7. Bake rolls in a preheated hot oven (400° F.) for 15–20 minutes.

24 rolls

---

* *The onion rolls can be frozen at this point. When ready to bake, place frozen rolls on a greased cookie sheet and let rise, uncovered, in warm place until doubled in bulk, about 1 hour. Then bake as directed.*

roll dough

2 packages active dry yeast
2 cups lukewarm water
1 cup whole eggs (about 4)
½ cup melted butter
½ cup sugar

1½ tablespoons salt
5–7 cups all-purpose flour
1 egg, well beaten, for wash
2 tablespoons poppy or
 caraway seeds

1. In a bowl soften yeast in lukewarm water. Stir in eggs, butter, sugar, salt and enough flour to form a stiff dough.

2. Knead on a floured surface until smooth and elastic, about 5 minutes. Place dough in a greased bowl and turn to grease top.

3. Let rise, covered, in a warm place until doubled in bulk, about 1 hour. Punch down and knead on a floured surface. Cut dough into 24 pieces.

4. Shape each piece into a smooth ball and place on a greased cookie sheet.

5. Flatten dough into rounds ½ inch thick.

6. With a sharp knife, slash top of round in a crisscross design 3 times.

7. Brush with egg wash and sprinkle with seeds.* Let rise until doubled in bulk, about 30 minutes.

8. Bake in a preheated hot oven (400° F.) for 15–20 minutes.

9. Serve warm.

24 rolls

---

* Rolls can be frozen at this point. When ready to bake, place frozen rolls on a greased cookie sheet and let rise in a warm place until doubled in bulk, about 1 hour. Then bake as directed.

egg bagels

2 packages active dry yeast	½ cup oil
¼ cup sugar	2 eggs
2 teaspoons salt	5–6 cups all-purpose flour
1½ cups lukewarm water	

1. In a bowl mix yeast, sugar and salt. Add water and stir until yeast is dissolved. Blend in oil and eggs. Stir in enough flour to form a stiff dough.

2. Knead dough on a floured surface until smooth and elastic. Place in a greased bowl and turn to grease top. Let rise, covered, in a warm place until doubled in bulk, about 1 hour.

3. Punch down, knead and cut dough into 18 pieces. Roll each piece into a long rope 11 inches long. Pinch ends together to form a ring.

4. Place rings on a cookie sheet and broil 1½ minutes on each side.

5. Drop rings into simmering water. Simmer for 5 minutes.

6. Drain thoroughly and place on greased cookie sheets.

7. Bake in a preheated moderate oven (350° F.) for 35–40 minutes, or until brown.*

8. Serve warm.

18 bagels

---

* *After baking, cool, wrap and freeze bagels. Use as needed. To reheat, place frozen bagels in a 350° F. oven for 5–6 minutes.*

challah

2 packages active dry yeast	7 tablespoons oil
⅔ cup lukewarm water	¼ cup sugar
⅓ cup egg yolks	2 teaspoons salt
(about 5–6)	4½–5 cups all-purpose
½ cup whole eggs	flour
(about 2–3)	1 egg, well beaten, for wash

1. In a large bowl soften yeast in water. Stir in egg yolks, whole eggs, oil, sugar and salt. Add enough flour to form a stiff, sticky dough.
2. Knead dough on a floured surface until smooth and elastic, about 5 minutes.
3. Place into a greased bowl and turn to grease top. Let rise, covered, in a warm place until doubled in bulk, about 2 hours.
4. Punch down, knead again and divide dough into 3 pieces. Roll each piece into a rope 12 inches long. Braid 3 ropes together and pinch ends to seal. Place on a greased cookie sheet.
5. Brush bread with egg wash and let rise, covered, in a warm place until doubled in bulk, about 45 minutes. Brush again with egg wash.
6. Bake in a preheated moderate oven (375° F.) for 35–40 minutes, or until richly browned.
7. Cool thoroughly on a rack before slicing.

1 loaf

raisin challah

1 recipe Challah dough	1 cup raisins
(see above)	

1. Prepare dough as directed, adding raisins to dough

when kneading. Blend the raisins into the dough thoroughly.

2. Shape and bake as directed.

spiral challah

1 recipe Challah dough
  (Page 106)

1. Prepare dough as directed.
2. Roll dough into a rope 24 inches long. Coil up into a spiral on a greased cookie sheet.
3. Bake as directed.

water challah

2 packages active dry yeast	1½ tablespoons salt
2 cups lukewarm water	1½ tablespoons sugar
1 egg	5–6 cups all-purpose flour
½ cup oil	1 egg, well beaten, for wash

1. In a bowl soften yeast in water. Stir in egg, oil, salt and sugar. Gradually add enough flour to form a stiff dough.
2. Knead dough on a floured surface until smooth and elastic, about 5 minutes.
3. Place dough in a greased bowl and turn to grease top. Let rise, covered, in a warm place until doubled in bulk, about 1 hour. Punch down, knead again and divide dough into 3 pieces.
4. Roll each piece into a rope 18 inches long. Braid 3 ropes together and pinch ends to seal.
5. Place on a greased cookie sheet. Brush with egg wash and let rise in a warm place until doubled in bulk, about 30 minutes.

6. Bake in a preheated moderate oven (375° F.) for 25 minutes. Brush with egg wash again and bake another 10 to 15 minutes, or until richly browned and loaf sounds hollow when tapped.

7. Cool thoroughly on a rack before slicing.

1 loaf

rye bread

2 packages active dry yeast
1½ cups lukewarm water
1½ cups lukewarm milk
¼ cup sugar
4 teaspoons salt
¼ cup oil
3 tablespoons caraway seeds
4 cups rye flour
5–6 cups all-purpose flour
1 egg, well beaten, for wash

1. In a bowl soften yeast in water. Stir in milk, sugar, salt, oil and caraway seeds. Blend in rye flour and enough all-purpose flour to form a stiff dough.

2. Knead dough on a floured surface until smooth and elastic, about 5 minutes. Place dough in a greased bowl and turn to grease top. Let rise, covered, in a warm place until doubled in bulk, about 1½ hours.

3. Punch down, knead on a floured surface and divide dough into 2 pieces. Roll out each piece into a 9 × 14-inch oblong.

4. Roll up each oblong like a jelly roll, starting at 14-inch side. Place on a greased cookie sheet. Brush with egg wash. Let rise, covered, until doubled in bulk, about 30 minutes.

5. Bake in a preheated moderate oven (375° F.) for 35–40 minutes.

6. Cool thoroughly on a rack before slicing.

2 loaves

pumpernickel bread

2 packages active dry yeast
2½ cups lukewarm water
1 tablespoon sugar
1 tablespoon salt
¼ cup oil
¼ cup molasses
¼ cup white vinegar
¼ cup cocoa

2 tablespoons caraway
 seeds, crushed
2 teaspoons instant coffee
2 teaspoons onion powder
1 teaspoon fennel seeds,
 crushed
4 cups rye flour
5½ cups all-purpose flour

1. In a large bowl soften yeast in water. Stir in sugar, salt, oil, molasses, vinegar, cocoa, caraway seeds, coffee, onion powder and fennel seeds. Gradually blend in rye flour and enough all-purpose flour to form a stiff dough.

2. Knead dough on a heavily floured surface until smooth and elastic, about 5 minutes. Place dough in a greased bowl and turn to grease top. Let rise, covered, in a warm place until doubled in bulk, about 1½ hours.

3. Punch down and knead on a floured board. Divide dough into 2 pieces. Shape each piece into a smooth ball.

4. Place dough into 2 greased 9-inch pie pans. Cut a crisscross in top of each. Let rise, covered in a warm place until doubled in bulk, about 30 minutes.

5. Bake in a preheated moderate oven (350° F.) for 45-50 minutes, or until loaves sound hollow when tapped.

6. Cool thoroughly on a rack before slicing.

2 round loaves

variation

Raisin Pumpernickel: Blend 2 cups of raisins into the dough in Step #1.

white bread

1 package active dry yeast	1¼ teaspoons salt
½ cup lukewarm water	¼ cup oil
½ cup lukewarm milk	2½–3 cups all-purpose flour
2 tablespoons sugar	

1. In a bowl soften yeast in water. Stir in milk, sugar, salt and oil. Stir in flour until a stiff dough is formed.

2. Knead dough on a floured surface until smooth and elastic, about 5 minutes. Place in a greased bowl and turn to grease top. Let rise, covered, in a warm place until doubled in bulk, about 1½ hours.

3. Punch down and knead dough on a floured surface. Roll dough out into a 9-inch square. Roll up like a jelly roll and place, seam side down, into a greased 9 × 5 × 3-inch loaf pan. Let rise, covered, until doubled in bulk, about 30 minutes.

4. Bake in a preheated moderate oven (375° F.) for 35–40 minutes, or until brown and loaf sounds hollow when tapped.

5. Cool thoroughly on a rack before slicing.

1 loaf

whole-wheat bread

1 package active dry yeast	¼ cup vegetable shortening
1¼ cups lukewarm water	1 cup lukewarm milk
⅓ cup sugar	2½ cups all-purpose flour
2 teaspoons salt	3 cups whole-wheat flour

1. In a large bowl soften yeast in ¼ cup lukewarm water.

2. Stir in sugar, salt, shortening, milk and remaining

1 cup lukewarm water. Stir in all-purpose flour and whole-wheat flour.

3. Turn dough onto a floured surface and knead until smooth and elastic, about 5 minutes. Place dough in a greased bowl and turn to grease top. Let rise, covered, in a warm place until doubled in bulk, about 1½ hours.

4. Punch down and knead on a floured surface. Divide dough into 2 pieces. Roll out each piece into a 9-inch square.

5. Roll up like a jelly roll and place, seam side down, into 2 greased 9 × 5 × 3-inch loaf pans. Let rise, covered, in a warm place until doubled in bulk, about 30 minutes.

6. Bake in a preheated hot oven (400° F.) for 40–45 minutes, or until loaves sound hollow when tapped.

7. Cool thoroughly on a rack before slicing.

2 loaves

crusty bread

2 packages active dry yeast
2 cups lukewarm water
1 tablespoon salt
1 tablespoon sugar
6 tablespoons vegetable shortening
5–5½ cups all-purpose flour

1. In a large bowl soften yeast in lukewarm water. Stir in salt, sugar, and shortening. Blend in enough flour to form a stiff, sticky dough.

2. Knead on a heavily floured surface until smooth and elastic, about 5 minutes. Place dough in a greased bowl and turn to grease top. Let rise, covered, in a warm place until doubled in bulk, about 1½ hours.

3. Punch down, knead again and divide dough into 3 pieces. Roll each piece into a 16 × 6-inch strip. Roll up at the 16-inch side into long rolls.

4. Slash top of each roll 4 or 5 times and place on a

greased cookie sheet. Brush tops of loaves with water and let rise, covered, in a warm place until doubled in bulk, about 30 minutes.

5. Place a shallow pan of water on bottom rack of a preheated hot oven (400° F.). Place bread loaves in oven and bake for 40–45 minutes, or until loaves sound hollow when tapped. Brush loaves with water every 15 minutes during baking.

6. Cool thoroughly on rack before slicing.

3 loaves

cheese bread

8 ounces (2 cups) sharp Cheddar cheese, shredded	2 teaspoons salt
2 cups milk	2 packages active dry yeast
2 tablespoons sugar	¼ cup lukewarm water
2 tablespoons vegetable shortening	5–5½ cups all-purpose flour

1. In a saucepan combine cheese, milk, sugar, shortening and salt. Cook, stirring over low heat until lukewarm.

2. Soften yeast in water and stir into cheese mixture.

3. Gradually stir in flour until a stiff dough is formed.

4. Turn dough out on a heavily floured surface and knead until smooth and elastic, about 5 minutes.

5. Place dough in a greased bowl and turn to grease all sides.

6. Let rise, covered, in a warm place until doubled in bulk, about 1 hour. Punch down and knead again.

7. Divide dough into 2 equal pieces. Roll out each piece on a floured surface to form a 9-inch square.

8. Roll up like a jelly roll and place, seam side down, into 2 greased 8½ × 4½ × 2½-inch loaf pans.

9. Let rise, covered, in a warm place until doubled in bulk, about 30–40 minutes.

10. Bake in a preheated moderate oven (375° F.) for 30–35 minutes, or until richly browned. Cool thoroughly on a rack before slicing.

2 loaves

banana nut bread

3 cups all-purpose flour, unsifted
3 teaspoons baking powder
¾ teaspoon salt
1 teaspoon baking soda
½ cup vegetable shortening
¾ cup brown sugar, firmly packed

3 eggs
1½ cups mashed ripe bananas (about 3)
Grated rind of 1 orange
1 cup coarsely chopped walnuts

1. Preheat oven to 350° F. (Moderate).
2. In a bowl combine flour, baking powder, salt, baking soda, shortening, sugar, eggs and bananas. Beat until smooth and well blended.
3. Fold in orange rind and walnuts.
4. Pour batter into a well-greased 9 × 5 × 3-inch loaf pan.
5. Bake for 40–45 minutes, or until firm to the touch. Unmold and cool thoroughly on a rack before slicing.

1 loaf

corn muffins

1 cup yellow cornmeal
1 cup all-purpose flour, unsifted
¼ cup sugar
½ teaspoon salt
4 teaspoons baking powder

1 egg
1 cup milk
¼ cup oil
½ teaspoon lemon extract
½ teaspoon vanilla extract

1. Preheat oven to 400° F. (Hot).
2. In a bowl combine cornmeal, flour, sugar, salt and baking powder. Add remaining ingredients and blend thoroughly.
3. Line muffin pan with cupcake papers. Fill cups three-fourths full with batter.
4. Bake for 15 minutes, or until golden brown.
5. Serve warm.

12 muffins

whole-wheat muffins

½ cup oil
¼ cup sugar
2 eggs
½ cup milk
1 tablespoon honey
1 cup all-purpose flour,
  unsifted

1 cup whole-wheat flour,
  unsifted
2 teaspoons baking powder
2 teaspoons baking soda
½ cup raisins

1. Preheat oven to 400° F. (Hot).
2. In a bowl mix oil, sugar, eggs, milk and honey.
3. Stir in remaining ingredients and blend thoroughly.
4. Line muffin pan with cupcake papers. Fill cups two-thirds full with batter.
5. Bake for 15 minutes, or until brown and firm.
6. Serve warm.

12 muffins

blueberry muffins

6 tablespoons vegetable
  shortening
½ cup sugar
2 small eggs
½ cup milk
1½ cups cake flour,
  unsifted

1 tablespoon baking powder
½ teaspoon salt
½ teaspoon vanilla extract
½ teaspoon lemon extract
1 cup blueberries, fresh or
  frozen dry-pack*

1. Preheat oven to 400° F. (Hot).
2. Cream shortening until light and fluffy. Add sugar. Beat in eggs and milk.
3. Stir in flour, baking powder, salt and extracts. Fold in blueberries.
4. Line muffin pan with cupcake papers. Fill cups two-thirds full with battter.
5. Bake for 20 minutes, or until richly browned.
6. Serve warm.

12 muffins

-----

* *Frozen blueberries do not have to be thawed before using.*

bran muffins

½ cup oil
¼ cup sugar
2 eggs
½ cup milk
1 tablespoon honey
1 cup all-purpose flour,
  unsifted

¾ cup whole-wheat flour,
  unsifted
¼ cup all-bran
2 teaspoons baking powder
2 teaspoons baking soda
½ cup raisins

1. Preheat oven to 400° F. (Hot).
2. In a bowl mix oil, sugar, eggs, milk and honey.
3. Stir in remaining ingredients and blend thoroughly.

4. Line muffin pan with cupcake papers. Fill cups two-thirds full with batter.

5. Bake for 15 minutes, or until brown and firm.

6. Serve warm.

12 muffins

Sandwiches

The sandwich was usually the choice of the indecisive diner. Faced with a number of choices on the menu, he winds up saying, in his confusion, "I'll just have a sandwich." Ratner's has eliminated the "just" from the sentence and has even added an exclamation point to the end. At Ratner's "I'll have a sandwich!" is said with anticipation rather than indecision.

Sandwiches can be open-faced or closed, single, double or triple deckered, hot or cold, filled with spreads or solids (or both), standard or improvised, large or small, thick or thin. All you need is a little courage and a big mouth, with or without onions.

Ratner's, in the heart of the breadlands, welcomes the sandwich back to respectability.

grilled lox and bagels

3 bagels, split
Butter

½ pound Nova Scotia lox, thinly sliced
1 small onion, chopped

1. Toast cut side of bagels slightly. Spread with butter.

2. Put slices of lox on each piece. Broil until the lox is slightly brown.

3. Sprinkle chopped onions over all.

Serves 3

COMBINATIONS

For each sandwich use 2 slices of desired bread.

Spread bread with soft butter and make sandwich combinations using the following fillings.

Add lettuce leaves and slices of tomato (optional) and serve with Coleslaw (Page 87), Potato Salad (Page 86) or Macaroni Salad (Page 88).

sardine and egg

Use skinless and boneless sardines and slices of hard-cooked egg (optional).

nova scotia salmon and cream cheese

Use thinly sliced Nova Scotia salmon. Spread bread with cream cheese and top with sliced salmon.

carp and lox

Use thinly sliced smoked carp and lox.

tuna

Use well drained tuna chunks or well-flaked tuna mixed with Blender Mayonnaise (Page 97).

egg

Use slices of hard-cooked egg and Blender Mayonnaise (Page 97) or Russian Dressing (Page 98).

chopped liver

Use Chopped Liver (Page 6) spread on bread. Sliced onions may be placed on top of the liver, if desired.

cheese

Use sliced American, Swiss, or Muenster cheese (cream cheese may be substituted).

For melted cheese make an American, Swiss or Muenster cheese sandwich. Heat butter in a skillet and sauté sandwich until brown on both sides and cheese is melted.

To make sandwich in a grill or waffle iron, prepare sandwich and spread outside with soft butter. Toast in grill or waffle iron until sandwich is brown.

tomato herring

Place several tomato herring fillets on bread.

chopped eggs and onions

Spread bread thickly with Chopped Eggs and Onions (Page 7).

western

Prepare Western Omelet as directed (Page 83). Fold omelet and place on bread slice. Serve hot.

canned salmon

Use canned, well-drained and flaked salmon mixed with Blender Mayonnaise (Page 97). Chopped Salmon and Celery (Page 9) may also be used.

smoked whitefish

Use slices of boneless smoked whitefish.

lettuce and tomato

Use lettuce leaves, washed and dried thoroughly, and thick slices of tomato. Salt to taste.

cream cheese and jelly

Eliminate soft butter on this sandwich. Spread bread thickly with cream cheese. Top cream cheese with desired jelly or preserves.

Pies and Pastries

NOTE: Disciples of Dr. Stillman, Weight Watchers and Assorted Dieters, skip the next three chapters.
NOTE: If you're none of the above, please don't drool on the paper.

Ratner's Pies and Pastries are the most extravagantly luscious concoctions ever devised; Strudel Apple or Cheese; Fruit pies (cherry, apple, pineapple); éclairs and cream puffs; elegant Danish pastries the Danes would gladly claim as their own (Butterhorns, Fingers, Cheese Pockets).

As Harry S. Truman once said, "If you can't stand the heat, stay out of the kitchen." If you can, take advantage of the labor-saving methods used at Ratner's. Many of the cake recipes are not mixed according to conventional methods. Wherever possible use an electric mixer or portable hand mixer unless we specify otherwise. Your batters and doughs will come out with a lighter and finer texture.

We wish you good flavor, beautiful fillings and not too much heat in the kitchen.

pie crust

2 cups all-purpose flour
½ teaspoon salt
⅔ cup vegetable shortening

⅓ cup ice water (approxi-
mately)

1. Preheat oven to 400° F. (Hot).
2. In a bowl mix flour and salt. Cut in shortening with a pastry blender until particles are very fine. Stir in water until dough leaves the sides of the bowl.
3. Knead dough a few times on a floured surface until smooth. Divide dough into 2 pieces.
4. Roll out dough on a floured surface to an 11-inch round. Place into an ungreased 9-inch pie pan. Fill with desired filling.
5. Roll out remaining crust. Place over filling. Trim excess crust and crimp edges. Prick top.
6. Bake for 35–40 minutes, or until crust is nicely browned.
7. Cool on rack.

One 9-inch double-crust pie

apple pie

1 recipe Pie Crust
   (see above)
2 (1-pound 4-ounce) cans
   pie-sliced apples, drained
   or 6 apples, peeled, cored
   and sliced

½ to 1 cup sugar (depend-
   ing on tartness of
   apples)
1 teaspoon cinnamon
1 teaspoon nutmeg
2 tablespoons butter

1. Prepare pie crust according to directions.
2. Combine remaining ingredients in a bowl and blend thoroughly.

3. Use as filling for pie crust.
4. Bake as directed for pie crust.

One 9-inch pie

blueberry pie

1 recipe Pie Crust
  (Page 122)
4 (10-ounce) packages
  frozen blueberries

1 envelope unflavored
  gelatin
½ cup sugar
¼ cup cornstarch

1. Prepare pie crust according to directions.
2. In a saucepan combine remaining ingredients. Cook over low heat until blueberries bubble and sauce thickens.
3. Cool.
4. Fill pie crust.
5. Bake as directed for pie crust.

One 9-inch pie

cherry pie

1 recipe Pie Crust
  (Page 122)
2 (1-pound) cans pitted
  sour cherries in water
1 envelope unflavored
  gelatin

½ cup sugar
¼ cup cornstarch
2 tablespoons butter
½ teaspoon almond extract

1. Prepare pie crust as directed.
2. In a saucepan combine remaining ingredients. Simmer until sauce becomes thick and bubbly.
3. Cool.

4. Fill pie crust.
5. Bake according to directions for pie crust.

One 9-inch pie

pineapple pie

1 recipe Pie Crust (Page 122)	1 envelope unflavored gelatin
2 (1-pound 4-ounce) cans crushed pineapple	¼ cup cornstarch
¼ cup sugar	2 tablespoons butter

1. Prepare pie crust as directed.
2. In a saucepan combine remaining ingredients. Simmer until sauce becomes thick and bubbly.
3. Cool.
4. Fill pie crust.
5. Bake as directed for pie crust.

NOTE: If desired, stir in ½ cup slivered almonds or chopped maraschino cherries.

One 9-inch pie

blueberry cheese pie

½ recipe Pie Crust (Page 122)	1 (1-pound 5-ounce) can blueberry pie filling
½ recipe Cheesecake Filling (Page 139)	

1. Preheat oven to 350° F. (Moderate).
2. Prepare pie crust according to directions making a high fluted edge all around the pie.
3. Prepare cheesecake filling according to directions and pour into pie shell.
4. Bake pie for 40 minutes. Cool on a rack.

5. When pie has thoroughly cooled, top with blueberry pie filling.

6. Refrigerate.

One 9-inch pie

basic strudel dough

DOUGH

1 cup lukewarm water
⅓ cup egg whites (about 2)
⅓ cup oil
¼ cup sugar
1 teaspoon salt
4½–5 cups all-purpose
    flour

Filling as desired
    (Pages 126–127)
¾ cup melted butter
1 cup corn flake crumbs
¼ cup ground nuts

1. Put all dough ingredients in a bowl and beat with an electric mixer until rubbery.

2. Knead on a floured surface for 10 minutes, or until smooth and elastic. Place in a greased bowl and turn to grease top. Let stand for 2 hours (this allows the dough to become stretchable).

3. Prepare desired filling.

4. Preheat oven to 375° F. (Moderate).

5. Place cloth or sheet on a table and dust with flour. Divide dough in half. Place 1 piece on cloth and roll out to a 12-inch square. Stretch carefully to a 26-inch square. (Pull dough gently from the outer edge, stretching the dough a little at a time, while working your way entirely around the dough. In this way a great deal of tearing is eliminated.) With a scissors, trim off thick edges. Repeat with remaining dough.

6. Brush with ¼ cup melted butter and sprinkle each with half the corn flake crumbs.

7. Lay filling out in a thin row along the side edge

of the dough. Using the cloth, lift dough and roll to cover filling. Turn in sides and continue rolling using cloth as an aid.

8. Roll strudel onto a greased cookie sheet. Brush with ¼ cup melted butter and sprinkle each with half the ground nuts.

9. Bake for 40 minutes, or until richly browned. Brush with remaining ¼ cup melted butter several times during baking.

10. Cool thoroughly on a rack and slice when lukewarm.

11. To recrisp strudel, place in 350° F. (Moderate) oven for 10 minutes.

2 strudels

fruit and nut filling

1 (15-ounce) package raisins
1 (8-ounce) package minced candied fruit
1 (4-ounce) can slivered almonds
1 cup orange marmalade
1 (8-ounce) package figs, chopped
1 (1-pound 4-ounce) can pie-sliced apples, drained

1. In a bowl combine all ingredients and blend thoroughly.
2. Use as filling for basic strudel dough (Page 125).

Filling for 2 strudels

apple filling

4 apples, sliced thin
1 cup sugar
1 (1-pound) can pitted sour red cherries, drained
1 teaspoon grated orange rind
1 teaspoon grated lemon rind
½ cup golden raisins
3 tablespoons cornstarch
½ cup corn flake crumbs
½ teaspoon cinnamon

1. In a bowl combine all ingredients and stir until well blended.

2. Use as filling for basic strudel dough (Page 125).

Filling for 2 strudels

cheese filling

1 pound farmer cheese	½ cup all-purpose flour
1 cup sugar	1 teaspoon vanilla extract
½ cup Clarified Butter (Page 96)	4 eggs
	1 cup golden raisins

1. In a bowl combine all ingredients except raisins and stir until well blended.

2. Add raisins and mix well.

3. Use as filling for basic strudel dough (Page 125).

Filling for 2 strudels

basic danish dough

1 package active dry yeast	1 cup whole eggs (about 4)
⅓ cup lukewarm milk	5½–6 cups all-purpose flour
½ teaspoon vanilla extract	2 cups (1 pound) unsalted
½ cup sugar	margarine, very cold

1. In a large bowl soften yeast in lukewarm milk.

2. Stir in vanilla, sugar and eggs. Add half the flour and beat with an electric mixer until very smooth. Add remaining flour gradually and beat until a stiff, sticky dough is formed.

3. Knead the dough on a lightly floured surface until smoth and elastic. Let dough rise, covered, in a warm dry place until doubled in bulk, about 1½ hours.

4. Punch down and knead again. Roll out to a 14-inch square.

5. Cut each margarine stick into 3 lengthwise slices. Place margarine on two-thirds of the dough. Fold uncovered third of dough over margarine. Fold other third over that.

6. Reroll dough to a 14-inch square and fold again into thirds. Wrap and chill for 30 minutes. Repeat.

7. Roll out and fold once more.

8. Shape as directed in recipes following.

fruit danish

1 recipe Basic Danish Dough (Page 127)	1 egg, well beaten, for wash
½ recipe Almond Mixture (See Butter Horns, Page 130)	1 (1-pound 5-ounce) can cherry, apple, pineapple, or blueberry pie filling

1. Prepare basic danish dough as directed.

2. Roll out dough to a 24-inch square. Spread thinly wth almond mixture. Fold dough into thirds.

3. Roll with a rolling pin until dough is 24 × 12 inches. Cut dough into ½-inch strips. Coil strips into pinwheels and place on a greased cookie sheet with sides.*

4. Brush pinwheels with egg wash and top with a tablespoonful of pie filling. Let rise, covered, until doubled in bulk, about 30 minutes.

5. Bake in a preheated moderate oven (370° F.) for 25 minutes, or until richly browned.

6. Cool on a rack. Delicious when served warm.

36 pastries

---

* It is preferable to use a cookie sheet with sides as this pastry tends to ooze butter and the sides prevent the butter from spilling onto the oven.

jam swirls

1 recipe Basic Danish
  Dough (Page 127)
1 cup apricot jam or any
  desired flavor

1 cup chopped nuts
1 egg, well beaten, for wash

1. Prepare basic danish dough as directed.
2. Combine jam and nuts.
3. Roll out dough to a 24-inch square. Spread thinly with jam and nut filling. Fold dough into thirds.
4. Roll dough with a rolling pin until 12 inches wide. Cut dough into ½-inch strips. Coil strips into pinwheels and place on a greased cookie sheet with sides.*
5. Brush with egg wash. Let rise, covered, until doubled in bulk, about 30 minutes.
6. Bake in a preheated moderate oven (375° F.) for 25 minutes, or until richly browned.
7. Cool on a rack. Delicious when served warm.

36 swirls

---

* It is preferable to use a cookie sheet with sides as this pastry tends to ooze butter and the sides prevent the butter from spilling onto the oven.

sugar spirals

1 recipe Basic Danish
  Dough (Page 127)
¼ cup melted butter

Sugar
1 egg, well beaten, for wash

1. Prepare basic danish dough as directed.
2. Roll dough out to a 24-inch square. Brush with butter and sprinkle with ½ cup sugar.
3. Roll up two opposite sides until rolls meet in the

center. Cut crosswise into ½-inch slices. Place slices, cut side up, on a greased cookie sheet with sides.* Brush spirals with egg wash and sprinkle with additional sugar. Let rise, covered, until doubled in bulk, about 30 minutes.

4. Bake in a preheated moderate oven (375° F.) for about 25 minutes, or until richly browned.

5. Cool on a rack. Delicious when served warm.

48 spirals

---

* *This pastry tends to ooze butter while baking and a pan with sides prevents the butter from dripping onto the oven.*

butter horns

1 recipe Basic Danish Dough (Page 127)	1 egg, well beaten, for wash

ALMOND MIXTURE

2 (8-ounce) cans almond paste	⅓ cup butter
1 cup sugar	⅓ cup water

STREUSEL

2 tablespoons shortening	¼ cup sugar
2 tablespoons butter	1 cup all-purpose flour

1. Prepare basic danish dough as directed.

2. Combine all almond mixture ingredients in a bowl and beat until smooth.

3. In another bowl mix streusel until crumbly.

4. Roll out dough on a floured surface to a 24-inch square. Spread with almond mixture and sprinkle with two-thirds of the streusel.

5. Cut dough into 4 strips. Cut each strip diagonally across into 10 triangles. Roll up triangles starting at side opposite point of triangle.

6. Place horns on a greased cookie sheet with sides,* about 3 inches apart. Brush with egg wash and let rise, covered, until doubled in bulk, about 30 minutes.

7. Sprinkle with remaining streusel and bake in a preheated moderate oven (375° F.) for 25 minutes, or until richly browned.

8. Cool on a rack.

40 horns

----

* *This pastry tends to ooze butter while baking and a cookie sheet with sides prevents the butter from dripping onto the oven.*

danish fingers

1 recipe Basic Danish Dough (Page 127)	1 cup chopped nuts
	1 cup raisins
1 cup apricot jam or other thick jam	1 egg, well beaten, for wash

1. Prepare basic danish dough as directed. Divide dough in half.

2. Roll out each piece on a floured surface to a 14 × 18-inch rectangle. Spread dough with jam and sprinkle with nuts and raisins.

3. Fold dough into thirds, shaping a piece 4 × 18 inches. Roll dough so it is 6 inches wide. Cut each piece into 16 strips. With a sharp knife cut one side of strip 5 times to notch.

4. Turn strip into a crescent and place on a greased cookie sheet with sides.* Brush crescents with egg wash and let rise, covered, in a warm place until doubled in bulk, about 30 minutes.

----

* *This pastry tends to ooze butter while baking and a pan with sides prevents the butter from dripping onto the oven.*

5. Bake in a preheated moderate oven (375° F.) for 25 minutes, or until richly browned.

6. Delicious when served warm.

32 fingers

cheese pockets

1 recipe Basic Danish
  Dough (Page 127)
1 pound farmer cheese
1 cup sugar
½ cup butter
½ cup all-purpose flour

¼ teaspoon salt
1 teaspoon vanilla extract
2 eggs
1 cup raisins
1 egg, well beaten, for wash

1. Prepare basic danish dough as directed.

2. On a floured surface roll out dough to a 24-inch square. Cut dough into 36 4-inch squares.

3. In a bowl mix cheese, sugar, butter, flour, salt, vanilla, eggs and raisins until well blended.

4. Top each square with cheese filling. Fold 4 corners to center and pinch points together.

5. Place on a greased cookie sheet that has sides.* Brush cheese pockets with egg and let rise, covered, until doubled in bulk, about 30 minutes.

6. Bake in a preheated moderate oven (375° F.) for 25 minutes, or until richly browned.

7. Cool on a rack.

36 pockets

------

* This pastry tends to ooze butter while baking and a pan with sides prevents the butter from dripping onto the oven.

miniature danish

DOUGH

1 cup butter	1⅓ cups sour cream
1 cup shortening	½ cup sugar
2 cups sifted cake flour	1 teaspoon vanilla
2 cups all-purpose flour	2 eggs

FILLING

1 (1-pound 5-ounce) can
  apple, cherry or blueberry
  pie filling

1. Combine all dough ingredients and beat until well blended.
2. Wrap dough and chill overnight.
3. Preheat oven to 350° F. (Moderate).
4. Divide dough into 4 pieces. Keep refrigerated until used. Roll out 1 piece at a time on a floured surface into a 12-inch square. Cut into 16 3-inch squares.
5. Top each square with a teaspoonful of desired filling. Fold two opposite corners over filling and press edges to seal.
6. Repeat process with remaining 3 pieces of dough.
7. Bake for 20–25 minutes, or until richly browned.
8. Cool on a rack.

64 pastries

miniature ruggeles

DOUGH

1 cup butter	¼ cup sugar
1 (8-ounce) package cream cheese	1 egg
1 cup sifted cake flour	1 teaspoon vanilla extract
1 cup all-purpose flour	½ teaspoon salt

FILLING

1 (12-ounce) jar apricot jam
2 cups raisins

2 cups finely chopped walnuts

1. Combine all dough ingredients in a bowl and mix with hands until a smooth ball is formed. Wrap dough and chill overnight.
2. Preheat oven to 375° F. (Moderate).
3. Divide dough into 2 pieces. Roll out each piece on a floured surface to a 16 × 20-inch rectangle. Spread with half the jam. Sprinkle with half the raisins and nuts.
4. Cut 16-inch side of dough into 4-inch strips. Cut strips into 10 triangles 2 inches wide at the base. Roll up the triangles starting at the side opposite the point.
5. Repeat with remaining dough and filling.
6. Place on greased cookie sheet and bake for 20–25 minutes, or until lightly brown.
7. Cool on a rack.

80 small ruggeles

cream puffs or éclairs

1 cup water
½ cup butter
1 cup all-purpose flour
4 eggs
Custard filling (Page 135)

Confectioners' sugar or Chocolate Butter Cream Frosting (optional) (Page 164)

1. Preheat oven to 400° F. (Hot).
2. In a saucepan bring water and butter to a boil. Add flour, all at once, and stir until dough forms a ball.
3. Cool for 5 minutes, then beat in eggs, one at a time, beating well after each addition. Texture should be smooth and shiny.

4. For cream puffs, spoon into mounds, 2 inches apart, on a greased cookie sheet. For éclairs, spoon into mounds 6 inches long and 1 inch wide. Bake for 45–50 minutes. Prick with a fork and return to oven for 5 minutes longer.

5. Cool thoroughly on a rack.

6. Slice off top and fill with custard. Replace top and sprinkle with confectioners' sugar or chocolate butter cream frosting.

12 large puffs or 12 éclairs

custard filling

½ cup sugar	2 cups milk
⅓ cup cornstarch	1 tablespoon vanilla extract
2 eggs	

1. In a saucepan mix sugar and cornstarch.

2. Stir in eggs and milk. Cook over low heat, stirring, until custard thickens.

3. Remove from heat. Cover (this prevents a skin from forming) and then chill.

4. Stir in vanilla extract and use to fill cream puffs or éclairs.

Cakes and Cookies

Choosing between cakes and cookies at Ratner's can be a problem. You have to decide whether you want heaven in small or large portions. That's not always as easy as it sounds, not when LARGE offers Chocolate layer cake, Cheesecake (strawberry, pineapple, blueberry, we've even got plain), Victory layer, Pound, Sponge, Honey, Coffee, Babka; and SMALL offers macaroons, checkerboard, buttons, Chinese, kuchel, bow ties, Taiglach.

There's a way out of the dilemma. Time. Start thinking about it now. Better than that, bake your own.

Start with the freshest, finest quality ingredients you can buy. You'll be in good shape, LARGE or SMALL.

As with pastries, use an electric or portable hand mixer. Standard measuring equipment is fine as long as you measure accurately. And if you're melting chocolate you can prevent scorching by doing it in a saucepan over hot water.

Can't miss.

almond sheet cake

½ recipe Basic Cookie Dough (Page 166)

FRANGIPANE FILLING

1 (8-ounce) can almond paste, crumbled
⅔ cup sugar
⅓ cup shortening
⅓ cup butter
2 large eggs
⅔ cup all-purpose flour
½ cup chopped candied fruit
1 cup chopped walnuts
1 cup apricot preserves

1. Preheat oven to 350° F. (Moderate).
2. Prepare cookie dough as directed. Press dough evenly into bottom and sides of an ungreased 15 × 10 × 1-inch pan. Bake for 10 minutes.
3. While cookie dough is baking, prepare frangipane filling. Beat almond paste, sugar, shortening, butter, eggs and flour with an electric mixer until smooth. Stir in fruit and nuts.
4. Spread preserves over cookie dough. Spread filling evenly over preserves.
5. Bake for 30 minutes longer, or until brown.
6. Cool thoroughly on a rack and then cut into squares.

One 15 × 10 × 1-inch cake

apple cake

½ recipe Basic Cookie Dough (Page 166)
1 (1-pound 4-ounce) can pie-sliced apples, drained
1 (1-pound 6-ounce) can lemon pie filling
1 (1-pound 4-ounce) can pineapple chunks, drained
1 cup raisins
1 teaspoon cinnamon
Vanilla ice cream or unsweetened whipped cream (optional)

STREUSEL

1 cup brown sugar, firmly packed	1 cup all-purpose flour
	½ cup (1 stick) butter

1. Preheat oven to 400° F. (Hot).
2. Prepare basic cookie dough as directed. Line the bottom and sides of an ungreased 15 × 10 × 1-inch baking pan with foil. Press dough into prepared pan with floured fingers.
3. In a bowl mix apples, pie filling, pineapple, raisins and cinnamon. Spread mixture into lined pan.
4. Prepare streusel by mixing sugar, flour and butter with fingers until crumbly. Sprinkle streusel mixture over fruit.
5. Bake for 45 minutes to 1 hour, or until richly browned.
6. Serve warm either plain or topped with scoops of vanilla ice cream or unsweetened whipped cream.

One 15 × 10 × 1-inch cake

banana cake

2 cups mashed very ripe bananas (about 4)	1 teaspoon baking soda
1¼ cups sugar	1 teaspoon baking powder
¾ cup shortening	1 cup milk
4 eggs	¼ cup all-purpose flour
3¼ cups cake flour	Confectioners' sugar

1. Preheat oven to 350° F. (Moderate).
2. In a bowl combine bananas and sugar. Add shortening and beat until well blended. Beat in eggs, one at a time, beating well after each addition.
3. Sift together the cake flour, baking soda and baking powder. Add to the banana mixture. Add the milk and all-purpose flour and mix together.

4. Pour into a greased 9 × 13 × 2-inch baking pan. Bake for 40–45 minutes.

5. Cool thoroughly on a rack. Dust with confectioners' sugar.

One 9 × 13-inch cake

cheesecake

½ recipe Basic Cookie Dough (Page 166)

Sugar (optional)

FILLING

1 pound cream cheese, at room temperature
1 pound farmer cheese
1⅓ cups sugar
6 tablespoons soft butter

1½ cups sour cream
3 tablespoons all-purpose flour
4 eggs
2 teaspoons vanilla extract

1. Preheat oven to 350° F. (Moderate).

2. Prepare cookie dough according to directions.

3. Press enough dough into an ungreased 9 × 13 × 2-inch baking pan to form a thin layer over the bottom and sides of the pan.*

4. To prepare filling, combine all ingredients and beat with an electric mixer until smooth.

5. Pour cheesecake filling into pan and bake for 1 hour. Cool on a rack.

6. If desired, when cheesecake has thoroughly cooled, sprinkle granulated sugar in a crisscross over the top of the cake.

One 9 × 13-inch cheesecake

---

* If there is any leftover dough, bake according to cookie dough recipe.

creamy cheesecake

1 pound sieved cottage
  cheese
1 (8-ounce) package cream
  cheese
¼ cup butter
6 tablespoons all-purpose
  flour

¼ cup non-fat dry milk
  crystals
1 cup sugar
4 eggs, separated
½ cup water

1. Preheat oven to 350° F. (Moderate).
2. In a bowl combine cheeses, butter, flour, milk crystals, ½ cup sugar, egg yolks and water. Beat with an electric mixer until smooth.
3. In another bowl beat egg whites until stiff but not dry. Gradually beat in remaining ½ cup sugar, 1 tablespoon at a time, until whites are stiff and glossy. Fold egg whites into cheese mixture.
4. Pour batter into a 10-inch spring-form pan. Bake for about 40 minutes, or until top is brown and firm.
5. Cool on a rack. Refrigerate.

One 10-inch cake

strawberry topping

½ cup strawberry jam
1 pint whole strawberries,
  hulled

½ cup apple jelly, heated

1. When cake has cooled, spread jam over top and stud with fresh strawberries.
2. Glaze with melted apple jelly.

pineapple filling

1 (3-ounce) package
  ladyfingers

½ cup pineapple preserves

1. Place ladyfingers on bottom of pan. Spread preserves over this and then fill with cheesecake mixture.

2. Bake according to directions.

chocolate chiffon layer cake

½ cup egg yolks (about 8)
½ cup oil
½ cup water
⅔ cup sugar
¼ teaspoon salt
2 cups sifted cake flour
1½ teaspoons baking powder
3 squares (3 ounces) unsweetened chocolate, melted

¾ cup egg whites (about 3–4)
¼ teaspoon cream of tartar
½ cup confectioners' sugar
Confectioners' sugar or Chocolate Butter Cream Frosting (Page 164), optional

1. Preheat oven to 350° F. (Moderate).

2. In a bowl beat egg yolks, oil, water, sugar, salt, flour, baking powder, and chocolate with an electric mixer until smooth.

3. In another bowl beat egg whites and cream of tartar until stiff. Gradually beat in confectioners' sugar and continue beating until glossy.

4. Fold egg whites into batter and pour into a greased and floured 15 × 10 × 1-inch loaf pan or 2 greased and floured 9-inch layer pans.

5. Bake for 25–30 minutes.

6. Unmold and cool on racks.

7. Serve plain with confectioners' sugar sprinkled on top or with chocolate butter cream frosting, if desired.

Two 9-inch layers or one loaf

chocolate cream cake

1 recipe Chocolate Chiffon
 Layer Cake (Page 141)
1 (3-ounce) package
 chocolate pudding and
 pie filling

2 cups milk
1 cup heavy cream,
 whipped
1½ cups finely crumbled
 chocolate wafers

1. Prepare batter for chocolate chiffon layer cake and bake in a 15 × 10 × 1-inch loaf pan according to directions.
2. Cool cake thoroughly. Trim crusts from cake and crumble finely. Cut cake into three 4 × 10-inch pieces.
3. Combine chocolate pudding and milk and stir over low heat until pudding thickens.
4. Cover (this prevents a skin from forming) and chill.
5. Fold in whipped cream.
6. Spread mixture between cake layers, sides and top.
7. Press crumbs against sides and top of cake.
8. Refrigerate until ready to serve.

One loaf

french coffeecake

1¼ cups sugar
1¼ cups shortening
3 eggs plus 2 egg whites
⅓ cup milk
⅓ cup almond paste
Dash of salt

1 teaspoon almond extract
2½ cups sifted cake flour
2½ teaspoons baking
 powder
1 cup macaroon crumbs

1. Preheat oven to 325° F. (Moderate).
2. With an electric mixer cream 1 cup sugar and shortening.

3. Beat in 3 eggs, milk, almond paste, salt and almond extract. Stir in flour and baking powder.

4. Beat 2 egg whites until stiff. Add ¼ cup sugar gradually, 1 tablespoon at a time, and continue beating until egg whites are stiff and glossy. Fold into batter.

5. Sprinkle macaroon crumbs on bottom of 9-inch ring pan. Pour cake mixture on top of the crumbs.

6. Bake for 1 hour.

7. Cool on a rack. Invert cake onto serving plate. Crumbs will be on top.

One 9-inch ring

honey cake

⅔ cup honey
⅓ cup sugar
2 teaspoons baking soda
¼ cup whole eggs
    (about 1–2)
¼ cup oil

¼ cup water
1 teaspoon cinnamon
1 teaspoon allspice
½ teaspoon salt
2 cups rye flour, unsifted

1. Preheat oven to 275° F. (Slow).

2. In a large bowl, combine all ingredients and beat with an electric mixer until smooth.

3. Line an ungreased 9 × 5 × 3-inch loaf pan with foil. Pour batter into pan.

4. Bake for 1½ hours, or until top is brown and cake is firm to the touch.

5. Cool on a rack.

One loaf cake

fruit honey cake

1 recipe Honey Cake
  (see above)

1 cup mixed candied fruits
  or raisins

1. Prepare batter for honey cake as directed.
2. Add candied fruits or raisins to batter and mix well.
3. Pour into a foil-lined ungreased 9 × 5 × 3-inch loaf pan and bake according to directions.

nut honey cake

1 recipe Honey Cake   1 cup quartered walnuts
(Page 143)

1. Prepare batter for honey cake as directed.
2. Add walnuts to batter and mix well.
3. Pour batter into a foil-lined ungreased 9 × 5 × 3-inch loaf pan and bake according to directions.

lemon chiffon cake

½ cup egg yolks (about 8)   1 teaspoon lemon extract
1 cup sugar   ¾ cup egg whites
½ cup oil   (about 3–4)
½ cup water   ¼ teaspoon cream of tartar
2½ cups sifted cake flour   Confectioners' sugar or
¼ teaspoon salt   Lemon Cream Fluff
1 teaspoon baking powder   (Page 165), optional

1. Preheat oven to 350° F. (Moderate).
2. In a bowl beat egg yolks, ½ cup sugar, oil, water, flour, salt, baking powder and lemon extract with an electric mixer until smooth.
3. In another bowl beat egg whites and cream of tartar until stiff. Gradually add remaining ½ cup sugar and continue beating until whites are stiff and glossy. Fold egg whites into batter.
4. Pour batter into 1 greased and floured 15 × 10 ×

1-inch loaf pan or two 9-inch layer pans. Bake for 25–30 minutes, or until golden brown.

5. Unmold and cool on racks.

6. May be served plain with confectioners' sugar sprinkled on top or with lemon cream fluff.

One loaf cake or two 9-inch layers

lemon cream cake

1 recipe Lemon Chiffon
Cake (Page 144)

1 recipe Lemon Cream
Fluff (Page 165)

1. Prepare cake batter and bake as directed in a 15 × 10 × 1-inch loaf pan.

2. After cake has cooled thoroughly, trim crusts and crumble finely. Cut cake into three 4 × 10-inch pieces.

3. Prepare lemon cream fluff according to directions.

4. Spread some of the fluff between the cake layers. Spread a thin layer over sides and top of cake.

5. Press crumbs against sides and top of cake.

6. Refrigerate until ready to serve.

One loaf cake

checkerboard cake

1 recipe Lemon Chiffon
Cake (Page 144)
2 squares (2 ounces) un-
sweetened chocolate,
melted

1 recipe Chocolate Butter
Cream Frosting
(Page 164)

1. Preheat oven to 350° F. (Moderate).

2. Prepare cake batter as directed. Spoon half the batter into a greased 9-inch square pan.

3. Stir chocolate into remaining batter and pour into a second greased 9-inch square pan.

4. Bake for 25–30 minutes.

5. Unmold and cool on racks.

6. With a sharp knife trim crusts from top, bottom and sides of each square so that white and dark layers are the same size. Cut each square into 8 strips.

7. Spread frosting on the side of a white strip and place on a platter. Place a chocolate strip next to the white strip and press together. Spread side of chocolate strip with frosting. Press a white strip next to chocolate one and press together. Spread side of white strip with frosting. Press a chocolate strip next to white one and press together.

8. Spread the top of the four strips with frosting.

9. Place another four strips as in the first layer, placing a chocolate strip over a white strip. Continue until you have 4 layers of cake. The end result will look like a checkerboard.

10. Spread top and sides of cake with remaining frosting.

11. Chill until ready to serve.

One loaf cake

seven layer cake

1 recipe Lemon Chiffon
Cake (Page 144)

1 recipe Chocolate Butter
Cream Frosting
(Page 164)

1. Preheat oven to 350° F. (Moderate).

2. Prepare cake batter as directed. Pour into a greased 11 × 4½ × 2¾-inch loaf pan and bake for 40–45 minutes, or until cake shrinks slightly from sides of pan and top feels firm to the touch.

3. Unmold and cool thoroughly on a rack.

4. Trim crusts off loaf and cut into 7 thin layers with a serrated knife, using a sawing motion.

5. Spread frosting thinly on each layer. Cover sides and top of cake with remaining frosting.

6. Chill until ready to serve.

One loaf cake

strawberry shortcake

1 recipe Lemon Chiffon Cake (Page 144)	(10 ounces each) frozen strawberries, thawed
2 pints strawberries, hulled and halved, or 4 packages	½ cup sugar
	1 cup heavy cream
	¼ cup confectioners' sugar

1. Prepare cake batter and bake as directed making two 9-inch layers.

2. Combine strawberries and sugar and let stand for 1 hour.

3. Spoon half the berries over one layer. Place second layer on top of berries and transfer to a cake platter.

4. Whip cream and confectioners' sugar until stiff. Spread cream over sides and top of cake. Place reserved strawberries on top of cake.

5. Chill until ready to serve.

One 9-inch layer cake

pound cake

1 cup sugar	½ teaspoon lemon extract
½ cup butter	½ teaspoon vanilla extract
½ cup shortening	4 eggs
¼ teaspoon salt	2 cups sifted cake flour
½ teaspoon rum flavoring	1 teaspoon baking powder

1. Preheat oven to 275° F. (Slow).

2. In a large bowl beat sugar, butter, shortening and salt until fluffy. Add rum flavoring and extracts.

3. Beat in eggs, one at a time, beating well after each addition. Gradually beat in flour and baking powder and continue beating until smooth and fluffy.

4. Spoon into a greased 9 × 5 × 3-inch loaf pan. Bake for 1¼ hours.

5. Unmold and cool on a rack.

One loaf cake

marble cake

1 recipe Pound Cake
  (Page 147)
4 squares (4 ounces) un-

sweetened chocolate,
melted

1. Preheat oven to 275° F. (Slow).

2. Prepare batter for pound cake as directed.

3. Divide batter into 2 parts. Stir melted chocolate into one part.

4. Spoon white batter into a greased 9 × 5 × 3-inch loaf pan. Drop spoonfuls of chocolate batter into white batter. Swirl chocolate into white with a spoon or knife.

5. Bake for 1¼ hours.

6. Unmold and cool on a rack.

One loaf cake

raisin cake

1 recipe Pound Cake
  (Page 147)
1 cup raisins

1 cup chopped walnuts
1 cup mixed candied fruits

1. Preheat oven to 275° F. (Slow).

2. Prepare pound cake batter as directed.

3. Add raisins, nuts and candied fruit to batter and blend thoroughly.

4. Bake in a greased 9 × 5 × 3-inch loaf pan for 1¼ hours.

5. Unmold and cool on a rack.

One loaf cake

sour cream loaf

1 cup sugar
½ cup butter
½ cup shortening
3 eggs
3 cups sifted cake flour
3 teaspoons baking powder
¼ teaspoon baking soda

¾ cup sour cream
½ cup chocolate chips
½ teaspoon cinnamon
1 tablespoon cocoa
½ cup crumbled lady-
    fingers

STREUSEL

½ cup brown sugar, firmly
    packed
⅓ cup all-purpose flour

3 tablespoons butter
½ cup slivered almonds

1. Preheat oven to 350° F. (Moderate).

2. In a bowl beat sugar, butter, shortening and eggs with an electric mixer. Add flour, baking powder, baking soda and sour cream. Beat until smooth.

3. Spread half the batter into a greased 11 × 4½ × 2¾-inch loaf pan. Sprinkle chocolate chips, cinnamon, cocoa and crumbled ladyfingers over the top.

4. Spoon over remaining batter, spreading it evenly.

5. In a bowl mix streusel ingredients until crumbly. Sprinkle over loaf.

6. Bake for 45 minutes, or until firm and brown.

7. Cool thoroughly on a rack before slicing.

One loaf cake

sponge cake

¼ cup egg yolks (about 4)
½ cup whole eggs
  (about 2)
½ cup sugar
1 cup cake flour
1 teaspoon baking powder

¼ teaspoon salt
1½ tablespoons warm
  water
2 teaspoons oil
½ teaspoon lemon extract
Confectioners' sugar

1. Preheat oven to 375° F. (Moderate).
2. In a large bowl beat egg yolks, whole eggs and sugar with an electric mixer to a spongy consistency.
3. Sift flour, baking powder and salt into a bowl. Pour egg mixture into flour and fold in thoroughly.
4. Combine water and oil. Fold into flour mixture. Add lemon extract and blend well.
5. Pour batter into a greased and floured 9 × 13 × 2-inch pan or two 8-inch layer pans. Bake for 25–30 minutes, or until lightly browned and firm to the touch.
6. Cool in pan on a rack and frost as desired.

One 8-inch layer cake

railroad cake

1 recipe Sponge Cake
  (see above)
1 (8-ounce) can almond
  paste
½ cup sugar

1 egg
1 (12-ounce) jar apricot
  preserves or other jam
½ cup chocolate sprinkles
1 cup slivered almonds

1. Preheat oven to 375° F. (Moderate).
2. Prepare sponge cake as directed. Bake in a greased 15 × 10 × 1-inch pan for 15–20 minutes. Remove cake from oven.
3. While cake is baking, beat almond paste, sugar and egg until smooth.

4. Spoon mixture in 6 bands down the length of the cake. Bake for 10 minutes longer. Cool.

5. Spoon jam between bands of almond paste mixture. Top with chocolate sprinkles and almonds.

6. To serve, cut into squares.

One 10 × 15-inch cake

ice cream cake

1 recipe Sponge Cake (Page 150)
½ pint *each* vanilla, chocolate and strawberry ice cream
Whipped Cream

1. Preheat oven to 375° F. (Moderate).

2. Prepare sponge cake according to directions.

3. Bake batter in 2 greased and floured 8-inch layer cake pans for 25–30 minutes, or until lightly browned. Unmold and cool thoroughly on racks.

4. Slice each into 2 thin layers, making a total of 4 layers. Spread ice cream on 3 of the layers (½ pint for each layer).

5. Top with remaining layer. Freeze and wrap when firm.

6. Remove from freezer 20 minutes before serving and decorate top with whipped cream.

One 8-inch layer cake

jelly roll

1 recipe Sponge Cake (Page 150)
1 (12-ounce) jar currant jelly
1 cup crumbled ladyfingers
Confectioners' sugar

1. Preheat oven to 375° F. (Moderate).

2. Prepare sponge cake according to directions.

3. Line a 10 × 15 × 1-inch jelly roll pan with foil and grease lightly. Bake for 15–20 minutes.

4. Turn cake out onto a towel sprinkled with sugar. Roll up cake in towel. Cool thoroughly on a rack.

5. Unroll and spread with half the jelly. Reroll.

6. Spread remaining jelly over top and sprinkle with crumbled ladyfingers. Sprinkle confectioners' sugar over the top.

One 10-inch jelly roll

victory layer cake

CAKE

2 cups sugar
4 cups sifted cake flour
1 tablespoon baking powder
1 tablespoon baking soda
½ teaspoon salt
1 cup shortening

4 squares (4 ounces) un-
  sweetened chocolate,
  melted
6 eggs
1 teaspoon vanilla extract
1½ cups milk

TOPPING

2 cups heavy cream,
  whipped

¼ cup confectioners' sugar
Chocolate Curls (Page 165)

1. Preheat oven to 350° F. (Moderate).

2. In a bowl mix all cake ingredients except eggs, vanilla and milk.

3. Beat in eggs, one at a time. Gradually beat in vanilla and milk.

4. Pour into 2 greased and floured 9-inch layer pans and bake for 35–40 minutes.

5. Unmold and cool on racks. Trim cake layers to make them level.

6. Whip cream and confectioners' sugar until stiff. Spread between layers and on top. Do not frost sides. Sprinkle with chocolate curls.

One 9-inch layer cake

brownies

2 cups sugar
½ cup all-purpose flour
1 cup vegetable shortening
1 cup cocoa
¼ cup water
½ teaspoon baking soda
Pinch of salt
½ teaspoon vanilla extract

1½ cups whole eggs
   (about 6)
2 cups sifted cake flour
½ cup milk
1 (8-ounce) can pecans or
   walnuts, chopped
Chocolate frosting or
   vanilla ice cream
   (optional)

1. Preheat oven to 350° F. (Moderate).
2. In a bowl cream sugar, all-purpose flour and shortening until smooth and fluffy.
3. Combine cocoa with water and add to batter. Beat in baking soda, salt, vanilla extract, eggs, cake flour and milk. Beat until smooth and fluffy. Fold in nuts.
4. Line a 15 × 10 × 1-inch jelly roll pan with foil (do not grease). Spread batter evenly in pan.
5. Bake for 30 minutes. Cool in pan on a rack.
6. Remove brownies from pan using foil. Turn upside down and peel off foil. Cut into bars or squares.
7. Brownies can be frosted with your favorite chocolate frosting or topped with scoops of vanilla ice cream.
One 15 × 10 × 1-inch pan

butterflies

½ cup whole eggs
   (about 2)
1¼ cups sugar
½ cup vegetable shortening
2 tablespoons baking
  powder

2 cups sifted cake flour
½ cup egg yolks (about 8)
⅔ cup milk
1 cup heavy cream
Confectioners' sugar

1. Preheat oven to 350° F. (Moderate).

2. In a large bowl, combine all ingredients except cream and confectioners' sugar. Beat with an electric mixer until smooth and well blended.

3. Line a muffin pan with cupcake papers. Fill cups with batter about two-thirds full.

4. Bake for 20 minutes, or until lightly browned. Remove from muffin pan and cool on a rack.

5. When ready to serve, slice each cupcake straight across the top. Cut each top into halves and reserve.

6. Whip cream and ¼ cup confectioners' sugar until stiff and top each cupcake with the cream.

7. Press the 2 reserved cupcake halves, cut side down, into cream to resemble a butterfly. Sprinkle with additional confectioners' sugar.

20 cupcakes

strawberry cupcakes

1 recipe Butterflies
  (Page 153)
1 cup apricot jam

Juice of ½ lemon
1 pint strawberries, hulled
  and halved

1. Prepare cupcakes as for butterflies. Bake and cool according to directions. Do not cut.

2. Heat jam and lemon juice in a saucepan until bubbly. Brush over cupcakes.

3. Top with strawberries cut side down. Spoon remaining jam mixture over top.

20 cupcakes

basic babka dough

1 package active dry yeast	1 teaspoon vanilla extract
⅔ cup lukewarm milk	½ teaspoon lemon extract
½ cup sugar	1 cup soft butter
1½ teaspoons salt	4½–5 cups all-purpose flour
1 cup whole eggs (about 4)	

1. In a large bowl soften yeast in milk. Stir in sugar, salt, eggs, extracts and butter. Beat well (mixture will be lumpy).
2. Add half the flour and beat with an electric mixer until smooth and thick.
3. Beat in remaining flour until a stiff dough is formed. Knead on a floured surface until smooth and elastic. Place dough in a greased bowl and turn to grease top. Let rise, covered, in a warm dry place for about 1½ hours. Punch down and shape as directed.
4. Let rise, covered, until doubled in bulk, about 30 minutes.
5. Bake as directed.

russian coffeecake

1 recipe Basic Babka
 Dough (see above)

ALMOND FILLING

2 (8-ounce) cans almond paste, crumbled	1 egg, well beaten, for wash
	1 cup chopped almonds
4 eggs	1 cup raisins
¼ cup sugar	1 teaspoon almond extract

1. Prepare babka dough as directed.
2. While dough is rising, beat almond paste, eggs

and sugar until smooth. Stir in nuts, raisins and almond extract.

3. Cut off one-third of the dough and roll on a floured surface to a 9 × 13-inch oblong. Place into a greased 9 × 13 × 2-inch baking pan. Spread with one-third of the almond paste.

4. Roll out remaining dough to a 13 × 21-inch oblong. Spread with remaining almond filling. Fold dough into thirds at the 21-inch side (dough will now be 13 × 7 inches).

5. Cut dough into 1-inch strips. Place strips, cut side up, on top of dough in pan, stretching strips of dough to fit 9-inch width of pan.

6. Brush with egg wash and let rise, covered, until doubled in bulk, about 30 minutes.

7. Bake in a preheated moderate oven (375° F.) for 45 minutes, or until richly browned.

8. Cool on a rack.

One coffeecake

babka loaf

1 recipe Basic Babka Dough (Page 155)
½ recipe Almond Filling

(See Russian Coffee Cake, Page 155)

1. Prepare babka dough as directed.

2. While dough is rising, prepare filling as directed.

3. Roll out dough on a floured surface to a 12 × 16-inch rectangle. Spread filling on rectangle.

4. Fold dough into thirds at the 16-inch side. Cut the dough crosswise into 6 strips. Roll each strip on a floured surface into a 12-inch roll.

5. Braid 3 rolls together and place in a greased 9 × 5 × 3-inch loaf pan. Let rise, covered, until doubled in bulk, about 30 minutes.

6. Bake in a preheated moderate oven (375° F.) for 30–35 minutes.

7. Unmold and cool thoroughly on a rack.

Two loaves

individual babkas

1 recipe Basic Babka Dough
  (Page 155)
1 (1-pound 5-ounce) can
  cherry, blueberry or pineapple pie filling

¼ cup melted butter
2 tablespoons sugar
¼ cup very finely chopped
  walnuts

1. Prepare babka dough as directed.

2. Line a muffin tin with cupcake paper.

3. Roll dough on a floured surface to a ¼-inch thickness. Cut dough with a floured cookie cutter into 4-inch rounds.

4. Top each round with a tablespoonful of filling.

5. Pull edges of dough up and around filling. Pinch edges together and place pinched ends down into a cupcake paper.

6. Brush tops with butter and sprinkle with sugar and nuts. Let rise, covered, until doubled in bulk, about 30 minutes.

7. Bake in a preheated moderate oven (375° F.) for 25–30 minutes.

8. Cool on a rack.

26 buns

muhn strips

1 recipe Basic Babka Dough
  (Page 155)

1 egg, well beaten, for wash
Poppy seeds

POPPY SEED FILLING

2 cups poppy seeds, ground in a blender	2 tablespoons honey
	Grated rind of 1 orange
1 cup milk	1 egg, well-beaten

1. Prepare babka dough as directed.
2. While dough is rising, prepare filling. Combine poppy seeds, milk, honey and orange rind in a saucepan. Simmer for 10 minutes.
3. Cool. Stir in egg.
4. Divide dough into 2 pieces. Roll out each piece on a floured surface to a 10 × 12-inch oblong. Spread dough with filling.
5. Fold dough into thirds at the 12-inch side (dough will now be 10 × 4 inches). Turn rolls over and place on 2 greased cookie sheets. Let rise, covered, until doubled in bulk, about 30 minutes.
6. Brush rolls with egg wash. Slash tops at 1-inch intervals and sprinkle with additional poppy seeds.
7. Bake in a preheated moderate oven (375° F.) for 35–40 minutes, or until richly browned.
8. Cool on racks.

2 strips

chocolate rolls

1 recipe Basic Babka Dough (Page 155)	1 egg, well beaten, for wash

FILLING

1 cup cocoa	1 cup chopped walnuts
⅔ cup sugar	1 cup raisins
½ cup milk	

1. Prepare babka dough as directed.
2. While dough is rising, combine cocoa, sugar, milk, walnuts and raisins in a bowl.

3. Divide dough into 2 pieces. Roll out each piece on a floured surface to a 10 × 12-inch oblong. Spread dough with filling.

4. Fold dough into thirds at the 12-inch side (dough will now be 10 × 4 inches). Turn rolls over and place on 2 greased cookie sheets. Slash tops of rolls at 1-inch intervals.

5. Brush tops of rolls with egg wash and let rise, covered, until doubled in bulk, about 30 minutes.

6. Bake in a preheated moderate oven (375° F.) for 35–40 minutes, or until richly browned.

7. Cool on racks.

2 rolls

blueberry pockets

1 recipe Basic Babka Dough (Page 155)
1 (1-pound 5-ounce) can blueberry pie filling

2 cups blueberries
1 egg, well beaten, for wash
Sugar

1. Prepare babka dough as directed.

2. In a bowl mix pie filling and blueberries.

3. Roll out dough on a floured surface to a 16 × 20-inch oblong. Cut dough into 4-inch squares.

4. Top each square with filling. Fold over, shaping a triangle and enclosing filling.

5. Place on greased cookie sheets. Brush with egg wash and sprinkle with sugar. Let rise, covered, until doubled in bulk, about 30 minutes.

6. Bake in a preheated moderate oven (375° F.) for 20–25 minutes, or until richly browned.

7. Cool thoroughly on racks.

20 pockets

hamantaschen I

½ recipe Basic Cookie   1 (17-ounce) jar prune
  Dough (Page 166)   butter*

1. Prepare cookie dough according to directions.
2. Preheat oven to 400° F. (Hot).
3. On a heavily floured surface roll out dough to a ¼-inch thickness. Cut dough into 4-inch rounds.
4. Top each round with a spoonful of prune butter. Fold towards center on 3 sides of the round, shaping like a triangle.
5. Bake on a greased cookie sheet for 15–20 minutes.
6. Cool on a rack.

16 pockets

---

* *To make prune butter, combine ½ pound pitted prunes, ½ cup sugar and 2 cups water in a saucepan. Simmer for 30–35 minutes, or until prunes are tender. Drain and press prunes through a sieve. Cool and use as filling.*

hamantaschen II

1 recipe Basic Babka Dough   1 egg, well beaten, for wash
  (Page 155)   Sugar
1 recipe Poppy Seed Filling
  (see Muhn Strips,
  Pages 157–158)

1. Prepare babka dough as directed.
2. Roll out on a floured surface to a ¼-inch thickness. Cut with a sharp knife into 20 4-inch squares.
3. Top each square with a tablespoonful of poppy seed filling. Fold over shaping a triangle and enclosing filling.

4. Place on greased cookie sheets. Brush with egg wash and sprinkle with sugar. Let rise, covered, until doubled in bulk, about 30 minutes.

5. Bake in a preheated moderate oven (375° F.) for 20–25 minutes, or until richly browned.

6. Cool thoroughly on racks.

20 pockets

mandelbreit

1 (8-ounce) can almond paste, crumbled
3 cups sugar
1½ teaspoons salt
1 cup butter
1 cup shortening
3 cups whole eggs (about 12)
12 cups all-purpose flour
¼ cup baking powder
1½ teaspoons vanilla extract
1 teaspoon almond extract
1 cup walnuts, coarsely chopped
¼ cup candied fruits
1 egg, well beaten, for wash
Sugar

FROSTING
1 cup cocoa
½ cup sugar
¼ cup water

1. In a large bowl combine almond paste, sugar, salt, butter, shortening and eggs. Beat until smooth.

2. Beat in flour, baking powder and extracts.

3. Place dough on a floured surface and knead a few times until a smooth ball is formed. Cut dough into 3 pieces.

4. Preheat oven to 375° F. (Moderate).

5. To prepare filling, mix cocoa, sugar and water in a bowl until a paste is formed.

6. Roll out 1 piece of dough to a 24 × 6-inch rectangle. Spoon paste in a long ribbon down the center of the dough. Wrap dough around filling and shape into a smooth roll. Cut roll into two 12-inch lengths and place on a greased cookie sheet about 4 inches apart.

7. Repeat with second piece of dough spreading with walnuts.

8. Repeat with third piece of dough spreading with candied fruits.

9. Brush all rolls with egg wash and sprinkle with additional sugar.

10. Bake the 6 rolls for 45 minutes, or until richly browned.

11. Cool on racks. Cut rolls into 1-inch pieces, slicing crosswise.

NOTE: Mandelbreit tastes even better after ageing for 1 week wrapped in foil. Slice after unwrapping.

Six 12-inch rolls

basic sweet roll dough

1 package active dry yeast
1 cup lukewarm milk
3 eggs
¼ cup sugar
Grated rind of ½ medium lemon
¼ cup butter
½ cup (4 ounces) farmer cheese
1½ teaspoons baking powder
4–5 cups all-purpose flour
1 egg, well beaten, for wash
Sugar

1. In a large bowl soften yeast in lukewarm milk. Stir in eggs, sugar, lemon rind, butter, cheese and baking powder. Stir in enough flour to form a stiff dough.

2. Turn dough out onto a floured surface and knead until smooth and elastic. Place dough in a greased bowl and turn to grease top. Let rise, covered, in a warm dry place until doubled in bulk, about 1½ hours. Punch down and shape.

3. Roll out half the dough on a floured surface to a ¼-inch thickness. Cut into 4-inch squares.

4. Top each square with 1 tablespoon desired filling (Pages 163–164).

5. Brush edges of square with water. Fold dough over filling. Brush with egg wash and sprinkle with sugar. Repeat with remaining dough.*

6. Let rise, covered, until doubled in bulk, about 30 minutes.

7. Bake in a preheated moderate oven (350° F.) for 25–30 minutes.

8. Cool thoroughly on a rack.

25 rolls

---

* *Dough may be wrapped and frozen at this point. When ready to bake, place on greased cookie sheets and let rise in a warm place until doubled in bulk, about 1 hour. Then bake according to directions.*

pineapple filling

2 (1-pound 5-ounce) cans
  pineapple pie filling

cheese filling

1 recipe Cheese Filling used
  for Blintzes (Page 67)

prune filling

1 (17-ounce) jar prune
  butter (or see Haman-
  taschen I, Page 160)

cherry filling

2 (1-pound 5-ounce) cans
  cherry pie filling

blueberry filling

2 (1-pound 5-ounce) cans
   blueberry pie filling

pinwheels

1 recipe Basic Sweet Roll   1 recipe Filling for Basic
   Dough (Page 162)   Sweet Roll (Pages 163–
                                      164)

1. Prepare roll dough as directed.
2. Cut 4-inch squares of dough diagonally from each corner to within 1 inch of the center.
3. Place 1 tablespoon filling in center.
4. Turn down half of each corner into the center of the bun to shape a pinwheel.*
5. Let rise, covered, until doubled in bulk, about 30 minutes.
6. Bake in a preheated moderate oven (350° F.) for 25–30 minutes.
7. Cool thoroughly on racks.

                                                      25 rolls

---

* Dough may be wrapped and frozen at this point. When ready to bake, place on greased cookie sheets and let rise in a warm place until doubled in bulk, about 1 hour. Then bake according to directions.

chocolate butter cream frosting

1 pound sifted confection-   2 teaspoons vanilla extract
   ers' sugar (4½ cups)   6 squares (ounces) semi-
2 cups butter or margarine   sweet chocolate, melted

1. Combine sugar, butter or margarine and vanilla. Add chocolate and beat until smooth.

2. Spread frosting between two 9-inch layers. Frost sides and top of cake.

Fills and frosts two 9-inch layers

lemon cream fluff

1 (3¼-ounce) package
  lemon pudding and pie
  filling

3 cups water
1 cup heavy cream,
  whipped

1. In a saucepan combine lemon pudding and water. Cook, stirring, over low heat until pudding thickens.

2. Cover (this prevents a skin from forming) and chill thoroughly.

3. Fold in whipped cream.

4. Use as filling and frosting for Lemon Cream Cake (Page 145) or Lemon Chiffon Cake (Page 144).

*Fills and frosts a Lemon Chiffon Cake or a
Lemon Cream Cake*

chocolate curls

Water
3 squares (3 ounces) semi-
  sweet chocolate

1. Make a small pan out of foil measuring 1½ × 2½ × ½ inches deep.

2. Melt chocolate in the top of a double boiler over the hot water.

3. Pour chocolate into foil pan and chill until firm.

4. Remove foil from chocolate and cut chocolate into long curls using a vegetable peeler.

5. Chill curls until ready to use as a garnish for cakes and cupcakes.

chocolate syrup

1 cup unsweetened cocoa	1 cup boiling water
2 cups sugar	2 teaspoons vanilla extract

1. Combine cocoa and sugar in a saucepan. Add boiling water and stir thoroughly.
2. Place saucepan on stove and bring to a boil while stirring, for about 3–5 minutes. Lower heat and simmer for 3 minutes longer.
3. Remove from heat. Add vanilla extract and cool.
4. Refrigerate and use as needed.

2½ cups

chocolate drink

8 ounces milk	Whipped Cream
2 tablespoons Chocolate Syrup (see above)	

1. Combine milk with chocolate syrup and blend thoroughly.
2. Serve topped with whipped cream.

1 serving

basic cookie dough

1 cup sugar	1 teaspoon vanilla extract
1 cup shortening	1 teaspoon lemon extract
1 cup butter	2 eggs
3 cups sifted cake flour	½ teaspoon salt
2 cups all-purpose flour	1 teaspoon baking powder

1. In a bowl combine all ingredients with the hands. Refrigerate for 3 or 4 hours, preferably overnight. (Dough may be wrapped and stored in the refrigerator for up to 2 weeks.)

2. Preheat oven to 375° F. (Moderate).

3. For plain cookies, roll dough out on a floured surface to a ¼-inch thickness. Cut with a floured cookie cutter into desired shapes.

4. Bake for 10–12 minutes, or until lightly browned.

5. Cool on racks.

About 8 dozen cookies (depending on size and shape)

buttons

2½ cups sugar	6 cups sifted cake flour
1 (8-ounce) can almond paste, crumbled	1 teaspoon almond extract
1¼ cups butter	Decorations: walnut quarters, red and green cherries, sprinkles
1¼ cups shortening	
1 cup egg yolks (about 10–12)	1 (12-ounce) package chocolate chips
1 cup whole eggs (about 4)	

1. Preheat oven to 350° F. (Moderate).

2. In a large bowl combine all the ingredients except the decorations and chocolate chips. Blend thoroughly.

3. Put half the dough into a pastry bag with a round hole tip and press out mounds the size of an olive, 2 inches apart, on greased cookie sheets. Press desired decorations on top of each rosette.

4. Bake for 10–15 minutes, or until lightly browned.

5. Stir chocolate chips into remaining dough.

6. Drop by heaping teaspoons, the size of an olive, onto greased cookie sheets and bake as above.

7. Cool all cookies on racks.

NOTE: If all chocolate chip cookies are desired, stir 2

(12-ounce) packages into dough and drop all the dough by teaspoons onto greased cookie sheets.

80 plain cookies and 80 chocolate chip cookies

checkerboard cookies

1 cup sugar
2 cups butter
6 cups sifted cake flour

½ cup egg yolks (about 8)
½ teaspoon vanilla extract
¼ cup cocoa

1. In a bowl combine all ingredients except cocoa. Beat with an electric mixer until crumbly.

2. Knead into a smooth ball and divide into 2 pieces. Knead cocoa into one half.

3. Roll out each piece of dough between 2 sheets of wax paper to a 10 × 14-inch oblong, ½ inch thick.

4. Using wax paper, place vanilla layer on top of chocolate layer. Carefully remove wax paper.

5. Cut oblong in half and place one on top of the other so there are 4 layers, white, chocolate, white and chocolate.

6. Cut the dough into ½-inch wide strips. Place 4 strips side by side with alternating strips so that the end of the strips form a checkerboard. Chill for 2 hours.

7. Preheat oven to 350° F. (Moderate).

8. Cut dough into ½-inch slices and place on a greased cookie sheet. Bake for 10–12 minutes, or until lightly browned.

9. Cool thoroughly on racks.

7 dozen

chinese cookies

2 cups sugar
2 cups shortening
6 cups all-purpose flour
3 eggs
1 teaspoon baking soda

¼ teaspoon salt
1 teaspoon vanilla extract
1 teaspoon almond extract
1½ cups chopped walnuts

FROSTING

2 cups confectioners' sugar
½ cup cocoa

Water

1. In a bowl combine sugar, shortening, flour, eggs, baking soda, salt and extracts. Beat with an electric mixer until crumbly.
2. Knead dough until a smooth ball is formed. Divide dough into 3 pieces and shape each piece into a long roll 1½ inches in diameter.
3. Roll each roll in nuts to coat the entire surface. Chill for 2 hours.
4. Preheat oven to 350° F. (Moderate).
5. Cut rolls into ½-inch slices. Place slices on greased cookie sheets.
6. Bake for 15 minutes, or until lightly browned. Cool on racks.
7. In a bowl prepare frosting. Mix confectioners' sugar and cocoa with enough water to achieve the consistency of heavy cream.
8. With a teaspoon spoon a tiny dab of frosting on each cookie.

8 dozen

chocolate chinese cookies

1 recipe Chinese Cookies (Page 169)	1 tablespoon sugar
	1 tablespoon water
2 tablespoons cocoa	Frosting (optional)

1. Prepare Chinese cookie dough as directed. Divide dough into 3 pieces and shape each piece into a 6 × 8-inch rectangle.

2. Combine cocoa, sugar and water and blend thoroughly.

3. Spread each piece of dough with cocoa mixture. Roll up and shape into a long roll 1½ inches in diameter.

4. Roll each roll in nuts to coat entire surface. Chill for 2 hours.

5. Preheat oven to 350° F. (Moderate).

6. Cut rolls into ½-inch slices. Place slices on greased cookie sheets.

7. Bake for 15 minutes, or until lightly browned. Cool on racks.

8. Serve plain or frost as directed for Chinese cookies.

8 dozen

macaroons

2 (8-ounce) cans almond paste	1 tablespoon orange gelatin powder
1 cup sugar	½ cup egg whites (about 2–3)
¼ cup all-purpose flour	
1 teaspoon lemon extract	¼ cup cocoa
1 teaspoon almond extract	1 tablespoon water

1. Preheat oven to 350° F. (Moderate).

2. In a bowl crumble almond paste. Add sugar, flour,

lemon extract, almond extract, orange gelatin and un-beaten egg whites. Beat with an electric mixer until smooth.

3. Place half of this mixture into a pastry bag with a wide opening star tip. Press out rosettes of dough about the size of a small walnut, about 2 inches apart, on a foil-lined cookie sheet.

4. Mix cocoa with water. Add to remaining dough. Press out chocolate rosettes as above.

5. Bake for 15–20 minutes, or until lightly browned and firm to the touch.

6. Cool thoroughly on racks.

38 macaroons (16 plain and 22 chocolate)*

---

* If you wish to make all plain macaroons, omit the cocoa and water. Makes 32 plain macaroons. If you wish to make all chocolate macaroons, add ½ cup cocoa and 2 tablespoons water. Makes 44 chocolate macroons.

passover nut cookies

1½ cups sugar
1 (8-ounce) can almond paste, crumbled
¾ cup butter
¾ cup shortening
1 cup egg whites (about 4–5)
1 pound shelled walnuts, ground

½ teaspoon salt
1½ teaspoons cinnamon
1½ teaspoons rum flavoring
½ teaspoon almond extract
1 (12-ounce) package matzoh meal
1½ teaspoons vanilla extract
¼ cup potato starch

1. Preheat oven to 350° F. (Moderate).
2. In a very large bowl combine sugar, almond paste, butter, shortening and unbeaten egg whites. Beat until well blended and fluffy.
3. Add remaining ingredients and stir until well blended.

4. Place dough into a pastry bag with a large star tip. Pipe out rosettes the size of small walnuts about 2 inches apart onto greased cookie sheets.

5. Bake for 15 minutes, or until lightly browned.

6. Cool thoroughly on racks.

7 dozen

refrigerator cookies

2 cups sugar
1 cup butter
1 cup shortening
3 eggs
1 tablespoon baking soda
3 cups unsifted all-purpose flour

3 cups unsifted cake flour
½ cup quick-cooking oatmeal
3 tablespoons chocolate sprinkles

1. In a bowl combine sugar, butter, shortening and eggs. Beat with an electric mixer until well blended and fluffy.

2. Add baking soda and flours. Beat until thoroughly mixed.

3. Turn dough out onto a floured surface and divide into 3 pieces. Roll 1 piece into a roll 12 inches long.

4. Knead oatmeal into second piece and shape into a 12-inch roll.

5. Knead chocolate sprinkles into third piece and shape into a roll 12 inches long.

6. Chill all 3 rolls overnight.

7. Preheat oven to 350° F. (Moderate).

8. Cut each roll into 36 slices and place on greased cookie sheets.

9. Bake for 15–20 minutes, or until golden brown. Cool on racks.

NOTE: These cookies may be made entirely plain or if all oatmeal cookies are desired, increase oatmeal used to 1½ cups and eliminate the chocolate sprinkles. If all cookies are to have chocolate sprinkles, increase the proportion to 9 tablespoons chocolate sprinkles and eliminate the oatmeal.

36 plain cookies, 36 oatmeal cookies and
36 cookies with chocolate sprinkles

bow ties

1 cup whole eggs (about 4)	2 tablespoons sugar
½ cup oil	2½ cups all-purpose flour
1 teaspoon rum flavoring	Additional sugar
½ teaspoon salt	

1. Combine all ingredients, except additional sugar, in a bowl and beat with an electric mixer for 5 minutes.

2. Allow dough to rest on a heavily floured surface for 30 minutes.

3. Preheat oven to 350° F. (Moderate).

4. Sprinkle additional sugar on a board and roll out the dough to ½-inch thickness. Cut into ¾-inch strips. Cut strips into 3-inch lengths. Twist like a bow tie.

5. Place on greased cookie sheets. Bake for 15–20 minutes, or until lightly browned.

6. Cool on racks.

3 dozen

egg kuchel

1 cup whole eggs (about 4)	½ teaspoon salt
½ cup oil	⅛ teaspoon ammonium
2 cups all-purpose flour	carbonate*
2 tablespoons sugar	Dash of white pepper

* Can be purchased in drug store or confectioners' supply house.

1. Preheat oven to 350° F. (Moderate).
2. In a bowl beat all ingredients with an electric mixer until thick, shiny and smooth.
3. Drop dough by teaspoons into mounds the size of small walnuts, 1½ inches apart, on a greased cookie sheet.
4. Bake for 20–25 minutes, or until lightly browned.
5. Cool on racks.
6. Store in an airtight container in a cool dry place.

4 dozen

sugar kuchel

1 cup whole eggs (about 4)	¼ teaspoon salt
½ cup oil	½ teaspoon vanilla extract
2 cups all-purpose flour	½ teaspoon rum flavoring
1 tablespoon sugar	Additional sugar

1. Combine all ingredients, except additional sugar, in a bowl and beat with an electric mixer until smooth and thick.
2. Turn out dough onto a heavily floured board. Sprinkle with flour and knead for 2 minutes until a smooth ball is formed. Let dough rest for 30 minutes.
3. Preheat oven to 400° F. (Hot).
4. Divide dough into 6 pieces. Roll each piece into flour. Roll out on a surface heavily sprinkled with additional sugar to form 9 × 7-inch oblongs.
5. Place oblongs on greased cookie sheets and sprinkle with more sugar. Press the dough down with fingertips so it will stick to the cookie sheet and not curl during baking.
6. Bake for 15 minutes, or until lightly browned.
7. Cool on a rack.

6 large kuchels

low-calorie kuchel

2 cups whole eggs
 (about 8)
1 cup oil
4 cups all-purpose flour
1 teaspoon rum flavoring

⅛ teaspoon ammonium
 carbonate*
2 tablespoons concentrated
 granular sugar substitute

1. Combine all ingredients in a bowl and beat with an electric mixer until a stiff dough is formed.
2. Place dough on a heavily floured surface and let rest for about 30 minutes.
3. Preheat oven to 400° F. (Hot).
4. Knead dough a few times and roll out to a ¼-inch thickness into an 18-inch square. Cut into 1½-inch squares.
5. Place squares on greased cookie sheets.
6. Bake for 15–20 minutes.
7. Cool on racks.
8. Store in an airtight container in a cool, dry place.
About 12 dozen

---

* *Can be purchased in drug store or confectioners' supply house.*

taiglach

DOUGH
2 cups whole eggs
 (about 8)
⅔ cup oil
1 tablespoon honey

1 tablespoon sugar
¼ teaspoon salt
5 cups all-purpose flour

COATING SYRUP

2 cups honey
2 cups sugar
1 (4-ounce) jar candied
  cherries

1 cup minced candied fruit
1 (8-ounce) can walnuts,
  coarsely chopped

1. Preheat oven to 400° F. (Hot).
2. In a bowl beat eggs, oil, honey, sugar, salt and flour with an electric mixer until smooth, thick and shiny.
3. Knead on a floured surface until smooth. Roll out to a ½-inch thickness. Cut into ½-inch strips. Cut strips into ½-inch pieces. Place on a greased cookie sheet.
4. Bake for about 10 minutes. Cool on a rack.
5. To prepare coating syrup, in a kettle place honey and sugar and stir over heat until temperature reaches 260° F. on a candy thermometer. Add cherries, fruits and nuts and stir thoroughly.
6. While syrup is hot, add pieces of baked dough and simmer for 5 minutes. Remove small amounts at a time with a slotted spoon and place on a greased cookie sheet in a thin layer.
7. Cool to lukewarm. With greased hands, shape taiglach into a large cone-shaped mound on a serving plate. Finished taiglach should resemble a pyramid.

Serves 10–12

Puddings and Fruit Desserts

Puddings require what Ratner's calls "attention to detail." None of Mother's "a little of this and a little of that." Not if you want what the inexperienced pudding maker never quite achieves . . . consistency. So check your Ben Franklins and make sure you're exact in following our instructions. Any idea what you'll come out with? Rice (hot or cold), Noodle, Matzoh, Bread, Indian puddings just like at Ratner's. And great Charlottes, too. Incidentally, if you're really insistent about topping some of them with ice cream or whipped cream, we won't stop you. As a matter of fact, we suggest it.

For variety, there's always the delightful fresh fruit standby, stewed fruits, peach Melba and anything you want to put together.

You can even give it your own name.

bread pudding

4 eggs
1 quart milk
½ cup sugar
¼ teaspoon salt
2 teaspoons vanilla extract
3 cups cubed Challah
   (Page 106)

1 teaspoon nutmeg
½ cup golden raisins
Cream or Fruit Sauce
   (Page 100), optional

1. Preheat oven to 350° F. (Moderate).
2. In a bowl beat eggs, milk, sugar, salt and vanilla extract.
3. Place challah cubes in a greased 9 × 13 × 2-inch pan. Sprinkle nutmeg and raisins over the bread. Pour egg mixture over all.
4. Bake for 40 minutes, or until pudding is puffed and brown.
5. Serve hot with cream or fruit sauce.

Serves 6

indian pudding

2 cups milk
2 cups heavy cream
¼ teaspoon salt
½ cup sugar
¾ cup yellow cornmeal
5 eggs

1 teaspoon grated orange
   rind
1 teaspoon vanilla extract
1 (1-pound) can cling
   peaches, drained and
   sliced

1. Preheat oven to 350° F. (Moderate).
2. In a saucepan combine milk, cream, salt, sugar and cornmeal. Bring to a boil and cook, stirring occasionally, until thick.

3. Beat eggs. Add orange rind and vanilla extract. Beat into hot cornmeal mixture. Stir in peaches.

4. Pour into a greased 2-quart casserole and bake for 1 hour, or until top of pudding browns slightly.

5. Serve warm.

Serves 6

matzoh pudding

4 matzohs	1 teaspoon grated orange
½ cup sugar	rind
4 eggs	½ cup golden raisins
1 pint half and half	1 (1-pound 14-ounce) can
2 cups milk	sliced cling peaches,
1 teaspoon vanilla extract	drained
Dash of salt	Fruit Sauce (Page 100),
	optional

1. Preheat oven to 350° F. (Moderate).

2. Soak matzohs in warm water to cover for about 5 minutes. Drain thoroughly and crumble.

3. In a bowl beat sugar, eggs, half and half, milk, vanilla extract and salt.

4. Combine matzohs, orange rind, raisins and peaches and place in a greased 9 × 12 × 2-inch baking pan. Pour egg mixture over all and stir to blend.

5. Bake for 40 minutes, or until pudding is puffed and brown.

6. Serve hot either plain or with warm Fruit Sauce.

Serves 6

noodle pudding

4 eggs
1 cup pot cheese, squeezed dry
⅔ cup half and half
⅓ cup milk
¼ cup sugar
½ teaspoon vanilla extract
1 teaspoon grated lemon rind
1 teaspoon grated orange rind
½ teaspoon cinnamon
1 (1-pound) can sliced peaches, drained
⅓ cup raisins
2 cups cooked broad noodles
Fruit Sauce (Page 100), optional

1. Preheat oven to 350° F. (Moderate).
2. In a bowl mix eggs, pot cheese, half and half, milk, sugar, vanilla extract, lemon and orange rinds and cinnamon. Blend well.
3. Place peaches, raisins and noodles into a greased 9-inch square pan. Pour batter over top.
4. Bake for 40–45 minutes, or until brown.
5. Serve hot either plain or topped with warm Fruit Sauce.

Serves 6

hot rice pudding

4 eggs
1 teaspoon vanilla extract
½ teaspoon salt
1 cup half and half
2 cups milk
3 cups cooked rice
½ cup sugar
1 teaspoon cinnamon
Cream (optional)

1. Preheat oven to 350° F. (Moderate).
2. In a medium bowl beat eggs. Add remaining ingredients, except cream, and mix thoroughly.

3. Pour mixture into a greased 9-inch square pan. Bake for 40–45 minutes, or until pudding browns slightly.

4. Serve warm with cream.

Serves 6–8

cold rice pudding

½ cup sugar	2 eggs
2 cups half and half	1 teaspoon vanilla extract
3 cups milk	2 tablespoons melted butter
3 cups cooked, drained rice	1 cup golden raisins
	Cinnamon

1. In a saucepan combine sugar, half and half, milk and rice. Cook, stirring occasionally, for 30 minutes.

2. Beat eggs. Put a small amount of hot mixture into eggs and then stir the eggs into the saucepan. (This prevents the eggs from curdling.)

3. Stir in vanilla extract, butter and raisins.

4. Pour mixture into individual serving dishes and sprinkle top with cinnamon.

5. Cool the rice pudding and refrigerate until ready to serve.

Serves 6–8

apple charlotte

½ recipe Basic Strudel Dough (Page 125) or packaged strudel leaves (12 × 16 sheets)*	1 (1-pound) can pitted sour red cherries
	Grated rind of 1 orange
½ cup melted butter	Grated rind of ½ lemon
½ cup corn flake crumbs	½ cup golden raisins
5 apples, peeled, cored and sliced thin	¼ cup cornstarch
1⅓ cups sugar	½ teaspoon cinnamon
	Sugar
	Vanilla ice cream (optional)

* If packaged strudel leaves are used, use 4 leaves for each charlotte, brushing each leaf with butter. Add filling and prepare as above.

1. Prepare strudel dough as directed. Stretch dough into a 20 × 28-inch oblong. Brush with some of the melted butter and sprinkle with corn flake crumbs.

2. Preheat oven to 350° F. (Moderate).

3. Combine apples, sugar, cherries, grated rinds, raisins, cornstarch and cinnamon.

4. Fold strudel sheet in half so it is 20 × 14 inches. Place on a greased cookie sheet. Pile filling 15 inches long down the length of the strudel dough.

5. Fold over ends and then fold over sides of dough so charlotte is 5 inches wide. Brush top with remaining butter and sprinkle with sugar.

6. Bake for 40–45 minutes, or until richly browned.

7. Cool on a rack until lukewarm. Cut into slices. May be served with scoops of vanilla ice cream.

1 charlotte

cheese charlotte

½ recipe Basic Strudel Dough (Page 125) or packaged strudel leaves (12 × 16 sheets) *
½ cup melted butter
½ cup corn flake crumbs
1½ pounds farmer cheese
1 cup sugar
½ cup butter
¼ cup all-purpose flour
2 teaspoons vanilla extract
4 eggs
1 teaspoon cinnamon
1½ cups raisins
Sugar

1. Prepare strudel dough as directed. Stretch dough into a 20 × 28-inch oblong. Brush with some of the melted butter and sprinkle with corn flake crumbs.

2. Preheat oven to 350° F. (Moderate).

3. Mix cheese, sugar, butter, flour, vanilla extract, eggs, and cinnamon until well blended. Stir in raisins.

4. Fold strudel sheet in half so it is 20 × 14 inches. Place on a greased cookie sheet. Pile filling 15 inches long down the length of the strudel dough.

5. Fold over ends and then fold over sides of dough so that they overlap on top. Charlotte will be about 5 inches wide. Brush top with remaining butter and sprinkle with sugar.

6. Bake for 40–45 minutes, or until richly browned.

7. Cool on a rack and then cut into slices.

1 charlotte

---

* *If packaged strudel leaves are used, use 4 leaves for each charlotte, brushing each leaf with butter. Add filling and prepare as above.*

baked apples

6 apples (Rome Beauty or Cortland)	1 cup water
1½ cups brown sugar, firmly packed	Cream (optional)

1. Preheat oven to 350° F. (Moderate).

2. Core apples and peel away tops.

3. Place apples in a pan side by side. Sprinkle with sugar. Add water to pan.

4. Bake apples for about 45 minutes, or until apples are easily pierced.

5. Serve warm or cold either plain or with cream.

Serves 6

applesauce

6 apples (McIntosh)	Cinnamon and nutmeg
½ cup sugar	(optional)
1 cup water	

1. Quarter unpeeled apples and place in a saucepan. Add sugar and water.

2. Cook apples until very soft, about 20 minutes. Add additional sugar to taste and cinnamon and nutmeg, if desired.

3. Strain mixture through a course sieve to separate the peelings and pits from the sauce. Sauce should be quite thick.

4. Chill.

Serves 6

variation

Applesauce can be combined with cranberry sauce (to taste) which has been cooked according to directions on package.

apple pancakes

5 eggs
¼ cup sugar
1½ cups milk
1 teaspoon vanilla extract
1½ cups all-purpose flour
½ teaspoon salt
1 teaspoon baking powder

2 cups peeled and finely shredded apples
Apple Filling (optional) (Page 185)
Confectioners' sugar
Syrup (optional)

1. Beat eggs, sugar, milk and vanilla in a bowl. Beat in enough flour to achieve the consistency of heavy cream. Stir in salt, baking powder and apples.

2. Grease a 7-inch skillet and pour in ⅓ cup batter. Brown evenly on both sides, turning once.

3. Spread filling on pancake, if desired.

4. Roll pancake and keep warm while preparing remaining pancakes.

5. Dust pancakes with confectioners' sugar and serve with syrup.

Twelve 7-inch pancakes

apple filling for apple pancakes

3 apples, peeled, cored and
chopped
½ cup sugar

1 teaspoon cinnamon
½ teaspoon nutmeg

1. Combine all ingredients and spread on apple pancakes as directed.

Filling for 1 recipe Apple Pancakes

apple or banana fritters

1 recipe Apple Pancakes
(Page 184), omitting
apples

6 apples, cored and peeled
OR 6 bananas
Oil for deep frying
Confectioners' sugar

1. Prepare batter for apple pancakes as directed.
2. If using apples, cut each apple into 8 wedges. If using bananas, cut each banana into 1-inch chunks.
3. Dip pieces of fruit into pancake batter and coat thoroughly.
4. Heat oil in a 10-inch skillet to 360° F. Drop coated fruit into oil and fry for 2–3 minutes, or until brown.
5. Drain fruit on absorbent paper. Sprinkle with confectioners' sugar.
6. Serve immediately.

Serves 6–8

stewed figs

18 dried figs
1 lemon, sliced

1½ cups heavy cream
(optional)

1. In a saucepan combine figs, lemon slices and water to cover about 1 inch above level of figs.

2. Cover and simmer for 30–35 minutes, or until figs are tender.

3. Cool and chill.

4. Serve plain or topped with heavy cream.

Serves 6

stewed prunes

1 (12-ounce) package pitted large prunes	1 lemon, sliced
¼ cup sugar	2 cups heavy cream

1. In a saucepan combine prunes, sugar and lemon slices. Add water to cover about 1 inch above level of prunes.

2. Cover and simmer for 20–25 minutes, or until prunes are tender.

3. Cool and chill.

4. Spoon prunes into serving dishes with some of the juice. Pour cream over the prunes and serve at once.

Serves 6

prune whip

1 (12-ounce) package pitted large prunes	1 lemon, sliced
¼ cup sugar	2 cups heavy cream, whipped

1. In a saucepan combine prunes, sugar and lemon slices. Add water to cover about 1 inch above level of prunes.

2. Cover and simmer for 20–25 minutes, or until

prunes are tender. Drain and reserve juice. Chill.

3. Remove lemon slices. Mash prunes until pulpy.

4. Fold whipped cream into prune mixture. Chill until ready to serve.

5. Serve in small dishes topped with some of the reserved juice.

Serves 6

fresh fruit cup

4 cups mixed fruit,* diced   4 tablespoons sugar
Lemon juice

1. Toss fruit with lemon juice to coat.

2. Divide fruit into 4 individual fruit cups. Sprinkle each with 1 tablespoon sugar.

3. Cover fruit and chill until ready to serve.

Serves 4

---

* This mixture can consist of the following fruits: apples, peeled and cored; pears; fresh pineapple; pitted cherries; peaches, peeled and pitted; apricots; nectarines, pitted; plums, pitted; bananas; grapefruit sections; orange sections; melon, peeled; grapes, stemmed and seeded; blueberries; blackberries; gooseberries; strawberries; raspberries.

peach melba

½ cling peach   or 2 tablespoons rasp-
Scoop of vanilla ice cream   berry preserves
¼ cup crushed raspberries

1. In a small serving dish place peach cut side up.

2. Top peach with vanilla ice cream.

3. Spoon raspberries or preserves over ice cream and serve at once.

1 serving

strawberry ice cream sundae*

Vanilla ice cream
¼ cup strawberries,
   crushed and sweetened

¼ cup heavy cream, sweet-
   ened and whipped
Chopped walnuts or pecans

1. Fill a parfait glass with vanilla ice cream.
2. Spoon strawberries into glass.
3. Top parfait with whipped cream and a sprinkling of chopped nuts.

1 serving

_____

* *Crushed pineapple or finely chopped canned peaches may be substituted for strawberries.*

Breakfast Menus

Fresh Orange Juice
French Toast* with Syrup or Jam
Coffee or Milk

Stewed Prunes*
Scrambled Eggs with Smoked Salmon and Onions*
Assorted Rolls and Butter
Coffee

Fresh Orange or Grapefruit Juice
Fried Matzohs served with Jelly or Applesauce*
Coffee

Stewed Figs*
Bagel* with Cream Cheese and Lox
Puffy Omelet*
Coffee

---

* For recipe, consult index.

Breakfast Menus

Grapefruit Half
Broiled Kippered Herring*
Mashed Potatoes with Fried Onions*
Rolls and Butter
Coffee

Melon
Oatmeal
Poached Eggs* on Toast
Coffee

Fruit Compote
Matzoh Meal Pancakes* served with Sour Cream
Coffee

---

* For recipe, consult index.

Lunch Menus (Supper)

Mushroom and Barley Soup*
Cheese and Fruit Blintzes* served with Sour Cream
Danish Pastries*
Coffee or Tea

Chopped Herring*
Pumpernickel Bread* and Butter Sandwiches
Sliced Tomatoes and Cucumbers
Baked Apple* with Cream
Coffee or Tea

Split Pea Soup*
Cheese Pancakes* with Applesauce* or Sour Cream
Fresh Fruit and Cookies
Coffee or Tea

Vegetable Plate (Any combination of Cooked
Vegetables)
Cheese Bread* and Butter
Strawberry Shortcake*
Coffee or Tea

---

* For recipe, consult index.

Spring Salad*
Bran Muffins* and Butter
Noodle Pudding served with Fruit Sauce*
Coffee or Tea

Vegetable Soup*
Crusty Bread* and Butter
Waldorf Salad*
Hot Rice Pudding*
Coffee

Salad Plate of Chopped Herring* and
Pickled Lox*
Lettuce, Sliced Tomato and Sliced Cucumber
Onion Rolls* and Butter
Cheese Pie*
Coffee or Tea

---

* For recipe, consult index.

Dinner Menus

Chopped Eggplant* Appetizer
Fricassee Balls with Gravy*
Mashed Potatoes
Pickled Beets and Cucumbers*
Fresh Fruit Cup*
Coffee or Tea

Matjes Herring
Lettuce and Sliced Tomatoes
Rye Bread* and Butter
Stuffed Cabbage*
Glazed Carrots* and Sweet and Sour Beets*
Apple Pie*
Coffee or Tea

Creamy Borscht*
Vegetable Cutlet* with Gravy*
Noodles with Butter
Sliced Orange Salad
Checkerboard Cake*
Coffee or Tea

---

* For recipe, consult index.

Cold Shav* with Chopped Raw Vegetables
Stuffed Flounder*
Baked Macaroni and Cheese* and Stringbeans
Danish Fingers*
Coffee or Tea

Potato Soup*
Broiled Fish, Italian Style*
Stewed Eggplant*
Iceberg Lettuce with Russian Dressing*
Apple Charlotte* and Whipped Cream
Coffee or Tea

Consommé with Matzoh Balls*
Baked Gefüllte Fish*
Barley with Onions*
Tossed Salad with French Dressing*
Raisin Challah*
Applesauce*   Honey Cake*   Sponge Cake*
Coffee or Tea

Consommé
Halibut Cantonese*
Egg Roll*   Brown Rice*
Fresh Fruit Cup*   Almond Cookies*
Tea

---

* *For recipe, consult index.*

Index